LITTLE ⊙

# 365
## Things to Do
## Before You
## Grow Up

Explore, discover,
try something new
every day!

Marc Tyler Nobleman

## STERLING

New York / London
www.sterlingpublishing.com/kids

STERLING and the distinctive Sterling logo are registered
trademarks of Sterling Publishing Co., Inc.

**Library of Congress Cataloging-in-Publication Data Available**

Lot #: 10/09
10  9  8  7  6  5  4  3  2  1

Published by Sterling Publishing Co., Inc.
387 Park Avenue South, New York, NY 10016
New text © 2010 by Marc Tyler Nobleman
Material in this book was previously published in 2000 as
*365 Adventures: Explore, discover, try something new every day*
and © Dutton Children's Books, a division of Penguin Putman Books
for Young Readers, 345 Hudson Street, New York, NY 10014.

Distributed in Canada by Sterling Publishing
*c*/o Canadian Manda Group, 165 Dufferin Street
Toronto, Ontario, Canada M6K 3H6
Distributed in the United Kingdom by GMC Distribution Services
Castle Place, 166 High Street, Lewes, East Sussex, England BN7 1XU
Distributed in Australia by Capricorn Link (Australia) Pty. Ltd.
P.O. Box 704, Windsor, NSW 2756, Australia

*Printed in China*
*All rights reserved.*

Sterling ISBN 978-1-4027-2968-3

For information about custom editions, special sales, premium and
corporate purchases, please contact Sterling Special Sales
Department at 800-805-5489 or specialsales@sterlingpublishing.com.

# CONTENTS

# #1. CELEBRATE Another Culture's Holiday

It's a long time from Independence Day in July until Labor Day in September. We could use a few more holidays in between, or any time of year. Why miss a chance to party?

Every country has its own customs and holidays, but they surely wouldn't mind a little international exposure. You'll have a blast introducing a foreign festival to America (or at least to your friends)!

You could acknowledge Children's Day (a holiday from the island nation of Vanuatu) in late July. Or Heroes' Day (a holiday from Zimbabwe) in August.

Most countries have their own Independence Day. Find out what some of them do to celebrate it, and celebrate the freedom of those faraway people on their special day. After all, that's what freedom is all about.

Any library should have a book or two on other cultures' holidays. Also, do a search for "international holidays" online; there are many good Web sites that list and explain them.

# #2. Plant a TREE

You've climbed its branches and sat in its shade, but have you ever planted a tree? Everyone should. Think of all trees do for us.

They give us oxygen to breathe. They are also the original air conditioners, providing shade in brutal summer heat. Their roots hold the soil in place so that it doesn't blow away. Hosts of mammals, birds, and insects call them home. When was the last time you really looked at a tree? They're beautiful.

Go to the library or a tree nursery to find out what kind of trees grow well in your area. Visit a garden center to buy a sapling. When you are ready to plant your new tree in the ground, make a day of it. Invite friends and have a tree-naming ceremony. Make time to visit the tree often and watch it grow. One day it might be big enough for you to sit under when it's too hot.

To find out more, visit the National Arbor Day Foundation's Web site at www.arborday.org.

# #3. Watch a METEOR Shower

Various meteor showers are annual events, as predictable as sunrise or sunset. People often gather to watch and make a party out of it. You don't even need a telescope.

A rocky or metallic chunk of space matter that has broken off from a planet or asteroid is called a meteoroid. Once it enters Earth's atmosphere, it is called a meteor, or shooting star, though it is not actually a star at all. Meteors often burn up as they approach Earth, but those that hit the ground are called meteorites.

Check your newspaper for the best date(s) to see them in your area.

---

### A few good meteor showers
#### (dates of best viewing in parentheses):

| | |
|---|---|
| Quadrantide: | December 28–January 7 (January 3) |
| Perseids: | July 23–August 22 (August 12); |
| Leonids: | November 14–20 (November 17) |
| Geminids: | December 7–15 (December 13) |

---

# #4. DONATE Stuff

If you really don't like cleaning up your room, there are two ways to avoid it: never let it get messy, or give away all your stuff so you don't have anything to clean up.

Okay, giving everything away is a bit drastic, but you can get rid of some of your belongings. Go through your closets and shelves and pull out the toys, books, and clothes you don't use anymore. Why let them contribute to the clutter? Give them to people who really need them.

Your town or city probably has more than one non-profit organization that can make sure your donation bag gets distributed properly. Call the Salvation Army or the American Red Cross, or maybe you know of another local cause. You don't have to donate only stuff—you can also donate your time. Find out if these organizations need any volunteers.

# #5. Find ANIMAL Tracks

If you live near a park or the woods, there are plenty of mysteries to solve. There are even mysteries in your own backyard!

What kinds of animals—wild or domestic—walked there recently? It may have happened late at night, when we weary humans were sleeping. Animals often are very active in the dark. (They're not as tired as we are, because they don't have to go to work or school all day.)

You don't even need a magnifying glass to hit the trails and track your furry or feathered friends—just your eyes. Go out for a walk early in the morning and see if you can find any evidence—footprints, droppings, leftover food—that an animal recently passed by. It's helpful to take along a guide to the local wildlife. Many books list the local animals and show pictures of what their footprints look like.

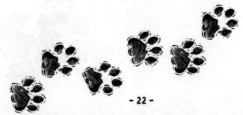

# #6. Change HANDS

Are you ambidextrous? This is not an insulting question—"ambidextrous" means you can easily use either your right or your left hand to do any task. So are you?

Most of us are either right-handed or left-handed, and do most tasks, such as dialing a phone, waving, and brushing our teeth, with that hand. If you're right-handed, try writing your name with your left. If you're left-handed, try it with the right. It will feel as if you've never written your name before.

Try to use only your opposite hand for an entire day. It's not as easy as you think. Opening the fridge, for example, might be a breeze, but using a fork or brushing your teeth may be downright frustrating. The more you practice, the better at it you'll become.

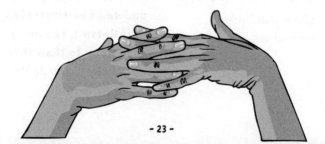

# #7. DRAW a Self-Portrait

Many great artists in history—Rembrandt, da Vinci, and Degas, just to name a few—have made pictures of themselves. You should be able to find some of their self-portraits in books or online.

Try to draw your self-portrait, even if you don't think you're artistic. Use any medium you like, such as pencils, paint, markers, chalk, pastels, or crayons. Or you can get really daring and try to create a sculpture out of clay. Looking in a mirror or referring to a photograph of yourself can be helpful.

Try different angles (profile, front, or even back). Try showing yourself smiling or just looking in the distance. You can also draw yourself as a character from your favorite book or movie. The possibilities are endless.

Your self-portrait does not have to look like you . . . and don't be frustrated if it doesn't. You don't even have to show it to anybody if you don't want to.

# #8. GROW a Salad

It wasn't too long ago that if you wanted something to eat, you had to grow it yourself.

Even though you are lucky enough to be able to buy your vegetables at a supermarket, why not plant a mini-garden and grow your own salad? Go to a nursery or library to find out what vegetables grow well in your area. You can order seeds at the nursery, or online.

If you don't have a yard, don't worry. All you need to grow a salad are a few pots, some soil, and sunshine. For planters, use anything that can hold dirt—big mugs, tin cans, old crates. Just water your plants and keep them in sunlight, and they won't know that they're not in a real garden!

Depending on what you choose to grow, you could have a full-fledged salad in a few weeks. Harvest your crops, rinse, add some dressing, and enjoy.

# #9. Keep a DREAM Journal

There is one place where you can fly, fight monsters, or show up at school in your underwear: in your dreams.

And there's one place you can write down all these wild exploits: in a dream journal. You may already have a diary, but a dream journal is a notebook you fill with what you dream about at night. Your dreams tell you a lot of things about yourself you didn't know!

You might notice recurring images, people, or feelings. You may even want to check out a dream analysis book to see what your dreams mean—but remember, they are just someone else's ideas, not facts.

Keep a notebook and a pencil by your bed. As soon as you wake up—even if it's in the middle of the night—write down anything you remember about your dream. Be sure to include as many details as you can. Since you won't remember most dreams past breakfast, don't put it off, no matter how busy you are! The more you write down your dreams, the more you'll be able to remember.

# #10. Do THREE Things That SCARE You

Fear can't hurt you. But missing an opportunity can.

Everyone is afraid of something. Does the thought of speaking to a crowd terrify you? Or does the idea of stepping onto an airplane make your knees weak? Make that fear work for you and get over it! You'll probably find that you are much braver than you think.

Make a list of your greatest fears and choose three that you'd like to try to conquer within a year. Take one fear at a time and try to make it less frightening. If you're afraid of speaking in front of others, practice in front of your family first, then a group of friends. If you're afraid of flying, look into airline statistics—it's actually very safe.

Take a deep breath, take your time, and believe in yourself. Don't be upset if you don't beat each fear. It's hard work and it takes a lot of strength. But don't give up before the year is over. And if you do triumph over all three, pick three more from your list for next year!

# #11. WRITE a Dog Dictionary

Although dogs (and other pets) can't talk, you can still understand what they are trying to tell you. The trick is being able to understand your pet's "language."

Does your dog scratch at the door whenever he wants to go out? Or does he bark three times when the mail carrier comes up the walk? Perhaps he sits in front of his bowl if he's hungry? This is your dog's way of communicating with you and letting you know what he wants and what he's thinking.

If you spend a lot of time with your dog, you probably understand his way of talking, but do your parents or your siblings? If your dog's actions leave your mom and dad scratching their heads and going "Huh?" then write a dog dictionary so they'll understand what your dog is trying to say. Not only will your dictionary help your family understand your dog a little better, but it could also be very helpful to a dog sitter or dog walker.

**woof \ adj**
**1: hungry**
**2: really hungry**
**3: tired**
**4: happy**
**5: really happy**

# #12. TAKE Fingerprints

Every time you touch something with your bare hand, you leave behind your very own "I was here" signature—your fingerprints.

No two people have the same fingerprints, and people's fingerprints never change as long as they live. The police and the FBI use fingerprints to identify crime suspects. British scientist Francis Galton first proposed fingerprinting as a method of identification and crime investigation in the 1880s. The people in your family probably aren't criminals, but you can still take their prints.

In your mind, round up the usual suspects—Mom, Dad, siblings. Make a "rap sheet" for each of them. Include their full name, birth date, eye color, hair color, height, and weight. Leave a blank box on the rap sheet for their fingerprint. Get a nontoxic ink stamp pad, or even a jar of finger paint, and ask everyone on your list to dab his or her thumb in the ink or the paint and then press it in the box on the rap sheet.

# #13. SPLATTER Your Shirts

Combine art, fashion, and business in seconds in your own backyard—create splatter art on your clothes.

Jackson Pollock (1912–1956) became a famous artist for creating huge canvases covered in splattered paint. You can make your own wearable, Pollock-esque masterpieces. Buy some plain white T-shirts. You can also use sweatshirts, but they're more expensive. You'll need fabric paint in lots of different colors, a brush, a cup of water, and an old sheet or a painter's drop cloth.

◉ Spread the sheet on the lawn and put the first shirt on it.

◉ Dip your brush in the paint, step back, and whip it at the shirt.

◉ Do this again with as many colors as you'd like. Then repeat and splatter paint on all the shirts. You'll be left with some pretty wild, colorful attire.

# #14. Be KIND to Strangers

Being kind to someone else—even someone you don't know—will not only make him or her happy, but it will make you feel good, too.

Everyone you pass on the street or in the school halls is a person with feelings just like you. Make a list of nice things you can do to lift people's spirits, then do one kind act a day for a week. It's not very hard, and you don't have to spend any money.

### Try these random acts of kindness:

◎ Thank someone who probably rarely gets thanked—a mail carrier, garbage collector, or bus driver.

◎ Hold the door open for people behind you.

◎ Donate clothes to a homeless shelter.

◎ Leave a flower on the grave of someone you never met.

◎ Tell someone that he or she has a nice smile.

◎ Carry an older person's groceries to his or her car or house.

# #15. CURE Hiccups

You don't need to—HIC—consult a shaman to cure the mystical affliction known as hiccups. They usually last only a few—HIC—minutes, whether we do anything or not.

What causes hiccups? Usually nothing more than minor stomach upsets or—HIC—eating too fast. Taking in carbon dioxide is what helps, and here are some methods to do that:

Lie on your back on a bed with your head hanging slightly over the edge. Breathe slowly. HIC. No?

Okay, the old familiar standby—breathe slowly into a small paper bag (but not for more than a minute). HIC. No?

Hold your breath. HIC. Try to cough a little. HIC. Gargle water. HIC.

If you still have the hiccups, you're a hard case. Drink a glass of water with one hand while pinching your nose shut with the other.

One of these methods should work. If not, by the time you're done trying them all, the hiccups probably will have gone away by themselves. HIC.

# #16. MAKE and BURY a Time Capsule

We've got plenty of easy ways to learn about the past—books, films, the Internet, word of mouth. Who wants to go dig up a box to do it? Kids in the future will.

A time capsule is some type of box (metal is best) that is filled with items from the current era and then buried for a future generation to enjoy.

Organize a time capsule project with your class at school. Include items that represent you and what your life is like. Put in photographs of yourself and your classmates, a newspaper, your favorite take-out menu, magazine ads, a popular book, a television guide—be creative.

Place all the items in the box along with a note explaining your choices. Ask a school administrator if you can bury it on school property, and leave a note in the main office that says "Time capsule from [teacher]'s class of [year]. Do Not Open Until [choose a year]." Go as far into the future as you want! Then forget about it…. Chances are you won't be around to see the reactions of the people who get to open it.

# #17. LEARN Another Language

Humans speak close to six thousand different languages. If you spoke them all, you could travel the world and never have to worry about understanding that strange sign on the train, or how to ask, "Where is the bathroom?" If you don't speak any other languages, wouldn't you like to learn?

The answer is yes! *Oui! Ja! Naam! Hai!* (in French, German, Swahili, and Japanese). You don't need to learn every language—learning one is a good start.

The most exciting way to learn any new language is by talking with people who are fluent in that language. If you don't know anyone who speaks the language you want to learn, you still have many options. You can use instructional books and multimedia on your own or learn with others by taking a class; many community colleges offer them. Or you can form a club with other kids who want to learn a language and practice together.

Chinese is the most widely spoken language in the world, followed by English, Hindi, Spanish, and Russian.

You'll be translating train signs in no time.

# #18. VISIT a Zoo at Feeding Time

Stop by the zoo at feeding time and find out what a rhino might consider a five-star meal.

Animals in zoos don't have to hunt for food the way their wild cousins do. Many animals, like sea lions and gorillas, have public feedings. A zookeeper comes out and feeds the animals in front of a crowd. Feeding time is an exciting time to visit your local zoo. Animals are more alert and more likely to put on a good show than at other times during the day.

Find out when your local zoo feeds its animals, and stop by to watch the show. Ask questions. The keepers know a lot and would be happy to tell you about their animals. You'll discover what tigers like to munch on and what makes crocodiles' mouths water. It isn't pizza! Mealworms, crickets, and raw meat may not make your tummy rumble, but to animals that's first-class cuisine.

# #19. TEST Your Memory

You probably have a good memory. You know your best friend's phone number by heart, your sister's birthday, and who the first president of the United States was. But your memory might not be as sharp as you think.

For example, what colors are on a traffic light? That's an easy one—green, red, and yellow.

But which color is on top? You probably see traffic lights every day, but don't be surprised if you don't remember that red is on top. It's not so easy!

Make a list of questions that test the power of people's observation of everyday life to ask your friends or family. Keep track of how many people know each answer. Ask them to create a list of similar questions to ask you.

---

### Try these:
**Does your school's front door open in or out?**

**What letters are on the "2" button on the telephone?**

**What color are your teacher's eyes?**

---

# #20. PRESS Flowers

Flowers look beautiful in many forms. It's just as nice to see a bountiful bouquet on a table as it is to find flowers growing along the road or in the woods, or to see them dried and preserved.

Dried, pressed flowers make great decorations. They can be hung on the wall, scattered delicately on a table, or used in any other display you think will brighten a room. You can also paste them onto construction paper to create an extra-special Valentine's Day, Mother's Day, or birthday card.

◎ Buy flowers that you like or pick them from your own garden. Tip: This does not include your neighbor's garden!

◎ Place the flowers between two sheets of paper, then place the "flower sandwich" between the pages of a big, heavy book. Pile more books on top if one book doesn't provide enough weight.

◎ Wait three to five days and open the book to see your newly pressed—and gorgeous—flowers. Repeat the procedure as often as you'd like.

# #21. Write a POEM

Poetry can sometimes get a bad "rap," but rap music itself—or any song, for that matter—is poetry.

Poems (1) don't have to rhyme, (2) don't have to be about serious things, and (3) can be any length. Now that you know that, you're very close to becoming an Unofficial Yet Absolutely Legitimate Poet!

You can write a poem about anything—your school, your family, your pets, your favorite memory, your angriest moment....

You can even write a poem about why you don't want to write a poem.

---

For inspiration, look through a book of poems or just listen to the radio. Pay attention to a song's words, not just the music. Of course, not all song lyrics are beautiful, but they usually have some poetic sense. You'll realize how many different forms a poem can take.

---

# #22. DRAW Your Great-Grandparents

Even if you never got the chance to meet your great-grandparents, it would be a wonderful experience to draw their portraits.

Maybe your family has old photographs of them. If not, that's where the real fun begins—you'll have to be a detective to find out exactly what your great-grandparents looked like.

Learn all you can about them. Ask your parents or grandparents or other relatives like aunts and uncles. Perhaps you can even track down some of their friends. Did they wear glasses? What color was their hair? Was it long or short? What kinds of clothes did they wear? Did they have a favorite outfit? Were they thin or not so thin? Ask as many questions as you want.

You can also look in history books to find out about the way of life in a certain town during the years when your great-grandparents lived there.

Then draw their pictures. It's quite an honor for them, and you'll feel like you got to know them a little better.

# #23. COMMUNICATE
## Without Speaking

Speaking is not the only way to get your point across. Watch five minutes of a movie with the sound off. Or observe people from a distance. You can probably understand a lot of what's going on just by watching their body language.

Find a patient partner with whom you can try this silent experiment. See how long you can spend time together without speaking. Try five minutes at first. Then ten. If you can go an hour, you will have quite a wonderful sense of accomplishment.

But don't just sit there! Do something active, so you're really challenged. Hike, pick apples, bake cookies, toss a ball, or wash a car.

Any time you wave, smile, frown, give a thumbs-up, tap your foot, or cross your arms, you're sending a message. These are only a few examples of gestures you can use to communicate.

# #24. RUN a Carnival

Putting on your own carnival is a great way to raise money for your school, club, or favorite charity.

Get permission to hold your carnival in the school parking lot, a local gym, or on part of your block. Make and post flyers announcing the upcoming event. Charge admission and sell popcorn, cookies, lemonade, and other goodies. Ask your friends and family to sign up to create and run a booth.

### Here are a few ideas for carnival games:

Go Fish—Glue small magnets to plastic fish and to strings attached to "fishing poles" (any stick will do). Put the fish in a kiddie pool filled with water, see who catches the most fish in thirty seconds, and give prizes to those people.

Penny Guess—Fill a clear jar with pennies (but count them first). Give a prize to the person whose guess is closest to the actual number of pennies in the jar.

Fortune-Telling—Write fortunes on slips of paper and put them in a "crystal ball" (use a glass bowl). Have someone dress up as a fortune-teller and "read" people's fortunes by pulling a slip from the bowl and reading it.

# #25. CONDUCT a TOUCH Test

It's time to get in touch with your senses. Conduct a touch test. Blindfold a volunteer, have him feel a variety of objects, and see if he can guess what he is touching.

Try an apple slice, a flower petal, a screw, a chess piece, a leaf, a sponge, a shoelace, oatmeal (cooked and uncooked), shaving cream, or anything else that's safe!

It's more fun if the object is taken out of context, the ring from a key chain, for example, or if it's different from what might be expected—like a peeled grape.

# #26. CONDUCT a SNIFF Test

When it comes to having fun, your nose knows how.

Together with a friend perform a series of sniff tests. While one of you is blindfolded, the other gathers a variety of things with distinct smells, such as a peeled banana, soap, salsa, grass, a sharpened pencil, or a leather glove.

Hold each sample under the tester's nose. The tester takes a whiff and tries to identify it. If the smell doesn't tell—oh, well! (Try again.)

# #27. LISTEN to Classical Music

Long before Beyoncé, Britney Spears, or even the Beatles, a few guys named Beethoven, Bach, and Mozart were rocking the music world.

Ludwig van Beethoven, Johann Sebastian Bach, and Wolfgang Amadeus Mozart are just three classical composers whose works are still wildly popular centuries after their deaths. There must be a reason. Find out for yourself. Classical music is more than just elevator music—it can be exhilarating, sad, thrilling, and soothing.

> You can find classical music on the radio, online, and at the library. Surprise your family by organizing a "classical music brunch" one Sunday— all you need are a few bagels and some CDs or MP3s.

# #28. TAKE an Animal Census

Creeping, crawling, hopping, flying, slithering, and lurking all around your neighborhood are two-legged, four-legged, and six-legged citizens—and that is not including humans!

Humans have invaded a lot of America's wilderness, but luckily we still have quite a few animals wandering about our cities and towns. Most stay out of our way, but a few are pesky. And at least a few probably wish that we'd stay out of their way.

One afternoon, take a census (a counting) of the animals in your neighborhood. How many squirrels, birds, insects, dogs, cats, and other animals can you count on your block?

If you encounter wild animals and pets you don't know, don't get too hands-on, especially if there are potentially dangerous animals like snakes or bears in your area.

Display your results in a report, on a poster, or on a Web site.

# #29. PARTY with Babies

Do you ever look at your baby pictures and think, "Is that diaper-wearing alien really me?" You've probably changed a lot since you wore diapers.

Do you think you'd be able to recognize your best friend as a baby? Throw a baby-photo party and find out. Ask each of your friends to bring a photograph of himself or herself under the age of two. Spread all of them out on a table or tape them to a big cardboard display, numbered underneath.

Pass out paper and pencils. Ask your friends to number their sheets and write their guesses for each baby. Then pick someone to give his or her guess for #1. Ask for a show of hands for all who agree. Finally, ask the former baby to reveal himself or herself. Repeat until all babies are identified.

You can give baby prizes for all correct first guesses (rattles, pacifiers, baby powder, or bottles). And serve only baby food!

# #30. RAISE Worms

Some of the best farmers are small, silent, and slimy. This isn't an insult—they're worms.

Worms help keep soil fertile so plants can grow. As worms burrow, they mix up the earth, allowing air and water to soak in. Worms are also decomposers (nature's way of recycling). They turn trash—like leaves, newspapers, and coffee grounds—into rich soil.

The worms will make usable soil from your garbage. When you're ready to retire from the worm-farming business, set them free in your garden or in a park.

**To start your own worm farm:**

1. Put some dirt in an old coffee can and add some worms (you can find them outside after rainstorms or buy them at a pet store).

2. Cover the worms with a layer of dirt (don't worry–they love it).

3. Add some coffee grounds, torn-up paper, and even more dirt.

4. Water your worms until the soil on top is soaked.

5. Cover the can with a lid, and store in a cool, dark place, like your garage.

"Manga" means print comics in Japanese. It's an art form whose popularity in America continues to grow.

Manga has a distinct look. People who like cartoons can easily identify the manga style at a glance. The visual symbols used in manga are often different from what we typically see in American comics.

For example, traditionally, American comics would show a character sleeping with eyes closed and perhaps a speech bubble with ZZZZs coming from his head. Manga style indicates a sleeping character with a bubble coming out of one nostril.

Check out a manga comic at the library or buy one. Then try your hand at drawing a manga-style comic strip of your own. Include as many manga symbols as you can. You can see a list of some of them at: en.wikipedia.org/wiki/Manga_iconography.

You can also experiment with converting an American strip that you like—superheroes, Saturday morning cartoons, Sunday comics, or anything else—to manga style.

# #32. TRACE Your Face

You've got your mom's eyes, your dad's nose, and your Uncle Bob's ears (lucky you!)—it's genetics!

Genetics is the field of scientific study that examines how physical and behavioral traits are transferred from parent to child. The term was coined in 1906. Look through old family photos and find out where your face comes from. Ask your parents, aunts and uncles, and grandparents if you can look through their photos. You're on a hunt for your own features. See how many people have eyes, a nose, a mouth, hair, or even ears like yours.

You can do the same with characteristics and behavior—find out from whom you got your laugh, your temper, and your smarts. You usually can't determine behavior from photos, but you can ask your parents and older relatives for the scoop.

## #33. PAN for Gold

In 1848, gold was discovered in California, spurring the Gold Rush. Although things have quieted down since then, there's still gold in them thar hills!

Gold is a precious metal that is easy to shape and is resistant to corrosion—that's why it's so valuable. You can find your own gold by panning in small streams, just like the forty-niners did back in the California Gold Rush. Some promising spots to try are South Dakota, Nevada, California, and the Southeast. For more specific areas, consult a tour book.

Scoop a few handfuls of sand and silt from the stream into your gold pan (it's not made of gold—it's used to find gold). Hold the pan underwater and move it gently in circles. Gold is heavy, so most of the lighter sediment will wash away while the gold sinks to the bottom. Lift the pan out of the water and swirl some more until the pan is almost empty.

See any gold flecks?

# #34. Investigate This Day in HISTORY

Pick a day that seems like nothing special. It will take only a few minutes to learn that *every* day is significant, or was, sometime in the past.

You can use your birthday, but it's also interesting to select a random day. Choose only a month and a day, not a specific year—you're searching for events that have happened on that date in many different years.

Look for history books that chronicle a decade, a century, or even a millennium, day by day. Your teacher or a librarian can help. Do an online search for "this day in history." There are many good sites that detail strange or historic occurrences on a day-by-day basis.

Ask older people you know if they've kept journals or diaries. If so, ask if they would share what they wrote on the day you picked.

> **Compile all the fascinating information you found and put it on the computer or on a big poster. Illustrate your findings and share them with your family and friends.**

# #35. Teach a DOG a TRICK

Think you can't teach an old dog a new trick? Think again!

Try teaching your dog to shake his paw. With the dog sitting, gently lift his right paw a few inches with your right hand and say "Shake." Gently shake the paw and repeat "Shake." Say "Good!" and pet him. Repeat this six times a day for three days.

On the fourth day, reach for the paw, but don't take it. If the dog lifts his paw, shake it gently and praise him. If he doesn't lift his paw, say "Shake." If he still doesn't lift his paw, repeat the original routine. He'll get it eventually.

**Animal training isn't easy. Keep these things in mind:**

**Always be kind and loving, and never get angry.**

**Praise your dog every time he does something right.**

**Have fun!**

# #36. OBSERVE Shadows

What comes between the sun and your shadow? You do!

Shadows are formed because sunlight does not bend around opaque (solid) objects. Instead, you see darkness in the shape of the object that is blocking the sun's light. As the sun moves across the sky, shadows get shorter or longer.

Decide what time of day you want to observe shadows. In the morning and late afternoon, shadows are longer than at midday. Pick a spot to keep a look-out. You might be most comfortable looking out your bedroom window. Or you can sit in a park, on a street bench, or anywhere else outside.

If you're a patient person, you could try for an hour of shadow watching. If you want, take photographs of the same object (a tree, a lamp, or a statue) every ten or fifteen minutes and write down the times you took them so you can label them when printed. You'll see the shadows move across the ground. You can also watch shadows creep along a wall, especially if you live in a city. Tall buildings cast shadows on other buildings.

How are things organized in your library? Don't be quick to say you don't have a library—the books you own are your library, even if you don't sign them out.

Take all the books off your shelf (unless they're already all over the floor). Decide how you want to reshelve them. You can use the Dewey Decimal System, which divides books into ten main classes, such as science, arts, and history/geography. Within these categories, books are alphabetized, often by the author's last name. You can get a list of the entire Dewey Decimal System online.

Or you can group them by different subjects than Dewey's.

Or you can also alphabetize your books without categories, just by title or by the author's last name.

You can even coordinate them by spine color; that would look nice but wouldn't make it easier to find what you're looking for.

Just don't leave them on the floor. Dewey—and your parents—wouldn't like that system.

# #38. DRAW from a Description

Police artists sketch suspects from descriptions alone. Witnesses tell the artist anything they remember about the culprit, and the artist turns it into a face— hopefully the right one.

Try it! Have a friend choose a person's photo from a magazine, but don't look at it yourself. Your friend must then describe the face to you, part by part, as you draw. It's not enough to say, "Two eyes, a nose, and a mouth." Make sure you get detailed information, such as, "Round, shiny eyes; a pointy, freckled nose; very thin lips." Get the hair, chin, ears, and eyebrows. Any tattoos or scars? Glasses? Braces? Nose rings?

When you're done, compare your drawing to the face. How accurate is your drawing? Was it your friend's description, your interpretation, your drawing ability, or teamwork that got the job done?

Try this with other things—an animal, a machine, a famous building. But keep the object a mystery to keep it a challenge. There's nothing to describe if you already know how it looks.

# #39. Break a RECORD

Somebody runs the fastest, grows the tallest, eats the most ... until someone else comes along and runs faster, grows taller, or eats more. You can be that someone.

Maybe you're good at jumping rope, milking cows, blowing bubbles, or building sand castles. Check out the *Guinness World Records* Web site (www.guinnessworldrecords.com) to see what you are up against. There are world records for everything from longest gum-wrapper chain to fastest sausage eater. Once you've decided what record you'd like to break, start practicing. Then practice some more. When you are ready to go for the record, make sure there are witnesses and video cameras around.

For a less global competition, organize a School Records competition. Include funny events such as "Shortest Attention Span" or "Hardest Last Name to Spell," along with more skill-oriented ones like "Most Cartwheels in a Row" or "Most Difficult Piece Played on the Piano." Try to have enough categories so that everyone wins something, then post the results in the school lobby.

# #40. Have a Surprise
# MOTHER'S DAY and FATHER'S DAY

Your mom wakes up on the second Sunday in May and knows that you're going to do something nice for her. Same with your dad, in June.

Imagine how surprised they'd be if you also did a nice thing on a morning in November. Or some afternoon in August. Sure, you do nice things for them all the time, but these would be extra-special occasions: a surprise Mother's Day and a surprise Father's Day.

If you have siblings, enlist their help. Pick two separate dates, one for your mom and one for your dad. Don't use consecutive days—make it more of a surprise and spread out the fun!

> **Plan something nice. Breakfast in bed is sweet.
> Picnics are fun. Write them a song and sing it.
> Do their chores for them.
> Babysit your younger siblings. Do whatever
> would make your mom and dad happy.**

Picking up things with your fingers is *so* easy. When was the last time you tried retrieving something with your toes?

We can grasp objects not just with our fingers, but also with our toes, or sandwiched between our forearm and upper arm, behind our knees, with a folded stomach, or depending on the object, with our mouths.

Mix it up for a little while. Pick up dropped items with your toes, arms, legs, or stomach. Have a contest with a sibling or friend to see who is faster at picking up an orange or apple in each of the four ways and then placing it in a basket. Dropping it is fine—as long as you don't pick it up again with your hands.

# #42. Create a MINIATURE Park

Create a park that is smaller than a parking space but that many people can still enjoy—just by looking at it, not strolling through it.

If you have a yard, ask your parents if you can use a small patch for your park. If not, ask friends, teachers, and others in your community to find a place where you could make one. Don't use any public (or private, for that matter) property without permission!

The size of the park is your choice, but you might want to keep your first park smaller than an average-size kitchen table.

Include any features you like in big parks. You can plant little shrubs as trees. Use gravel or dirt to make a walking or running path around the park. Dig a hole in the center, line it with aluminum foil or a plastic tub, and fill it with water to create a small pond. If you want, buy little benches or playground equipment. These things are usually available at stores where dollhouses are sold, or even at some toy stores.

Name your park and display that name on a small sign at its entrance.

# #43. Make MNEMONICS

A mnemonic is a sequence or sentence that you create to remember lists.

Here's a mnemonic that might help you remember the eight planets in order:

**Monkeys vacuum every morning joyously singing until noon.**

**M**onkeys (Mercury)        **J**oyously (Jupiter)
**V**acuum (Venus)           **S**inging (Saturn)
**E**very (Earth)            **U**ntil (Uranus)
**M**orning (Mars)           **N**oon (Neptune)

It's nonsense, right?

Create a few mnemonics. Your lists don't have to be for a fixed group, like planets. For example, if you want to remember a short shopping list:

**Big kites may look attractive.**

**b**read                    **l**ettuce
**k**etchup                  **a**pples
**m**ilk

# #44. SLEEP Outside

Have you ever lain on the grass to watch fireworks, listen to an outdoor concert, or take a break from eating at a picnic? It's comfortable. So comfortable you might have even dozed off.

Sleeping outdoors overnight is a pleasure that many people don't get to experience in our modern world. If you pick a night that's not too cold or too warm and find a safe, soft spot somewhere, you could enjoy a very peaceful night's rest. You need only a sleeping bag (tent optional), family or friends, a clear sky, and maybe a campfire.

Your backyard might do nicely, or you and an adult can research local campgrounds and pick one that sounds good.

Our prehistoric ancestors slept on the ground year-round. Of course, they had no choice—beds hadn't been invented yet.

You do have a choice—so choose a night and fall asleep under the stars

# #45. Take a LEAF Survey

Even if it doesn't look like it at first, leaves can be as different as people. Go on a leaf hunt and find out how different the leaves are in your neighborhood.

You'll find leaves with ragged edges and with rounded edges; some that are green, some yellowish, and some brownish; some shiny, and some dull; some oval-shaped, some star-shaped, and some in shapes there's no word for.

Glue your leaves into a notebook, one leaf per page. Below each leaf, write where you found it and what type of tree it's from. Your library will have a tree guidebook to help you identify which leaf is which, or you can use a well-researched Web site.

# #46. LEARN to Use Chopsticks

Do you remember your first fork lesson? Probably not, but you will remember your first chopstick lesson. Chopsticks are essential utensils in many Asian countries. In some, you couldn't find a fork if you looked all day!

Chopsticks are simply two slender sticks, a little longer than a pencil, commonly made of wood. People have used them to lift food to the mouth since ancient times, when chopsticks were often made of bone.

For your first chopstick experience, go to an Asian restaurant (Chinese, Japanese, Vietnamese, or Korean). The chopsticks will probably already be on the table. Using the hand you write with, grasp a stick with your thumb and index finger, as if it were a pencil. Rest the other stick at the base of the inside of your thumb and along your middle or ring finger. Hold this bottom stick steady and move the top one up and down to grab things.

Don't worry if you don't get it right away—it can take a lot of practice. You can ask someone at the restaurant to give you pointers.

# #47. RUN a Pet Show

Who's got the cutest cat on your block? Or the most talented dog? Organize a neighborhood pet show and find out!

Most people are proud of their pets and welcome any opportunity to show them off, and a pet show is the perfect place. Choose a date and reserve a location for your show. If it's summer, have it in someone's yard. If it's winter or you're worried about rain, hold it in a basement or garage.

Most important, get your participants! Circulate a flyer in school or in the neighborhood (or send an e-mail to people you know) announcing the show. Include competition categories like Fattest Cat, Best Dog Trick, Fastest Turtle. Try to create enough categories so that every pet can win one, or you can award first, second, and third place prizes in fewer categories. Ask three to five people (whose pets are not in the show) to be judges, and ask someone else to videotape the show. Make sure there is plenty of water on hand for the pets.

Let the competition begin!

# #48. LIVE in a Different Time Zone

When people in New York are eating lunch, people in California are just eating breakfast. They didn't oversleep—they live in a different time zone.

Earth has twenty-four time zones, and there are four in the United States (not including Alaska and Hawaii): eastern, central, mountain, and Pacific standard time. Central is one hour earlier than eastern. Mountain is two hours earlier, and Pacific is three. So when it is 12 noon in New York, it is 11 AM in Chicago, 10 AM in Denver, and 9 AM in Los Angeles.

Pick a time zone other than your own and spend a day on that schedule. It's best to do this on a weekend or a vacation day so you don't have to explain to your teachers why you're so late (or early) for class. Set your alarm, wake up, eat breakfast, lunch, and dinner, and then go to bed according to the alternate time zone. It's not exactly time travel, but it's the next best thing.

# #49. TEST Gravity

Gravity is man, woman, and animal's best friend. Without it, we would all drift into space.

Many of us tested gravity before we could talk or walk. When a baby throws a cup (and laughs as it hits the floor), the young scientist is experimenting with gravity, the force that pulls objects toward one another. That's why the cup falls instead of floating in the air. But which falls faster, a penny or a brick? What about a brick or a boulder? They all fall at the same rate. Gravity pulls them to Earth with the same force, regardless of weight or size.

Take several objects of different weights (nothing sharp or breakable!) and find a place outdoors to test gravity. Try a porch or a staircase, but just make sure no one and nothing are directly below! Have a friend watch from the ground as you drop any two items. Did they land at the same time?

# #50. MAKE a Candle

Before the lightbulb was invented, people lit up their homes with candles and kerosene lamps. Make yourself a candle and spend a night the way people did in the old days—with no electricity (that means no TV, too!). To make a candle, you'll need an adult assistant, a candle mold, some beeswax, and a cotton string for the wick—all of which you can get at a crafts store (except for the adult!).

1. Melt the wax in the upper tray of a double boiler (a two-level pan that keeps things from getting too hot), because the wax could flare up under direct heat. Do NOT boil the wax, just melt it.

2. Cut a piece of wick, and lower the string until one end reaches the bottom of the candle mold. Make sure it's long enough to stick up out of the mold.

3. Holding the wick in place, supervise your adult as he or she carefully pours the hot wax into the mold, right up to the top.

4. Let it cool, peel off the mold, and light up the night.

# #51. DO the DIALOGUE

Gather your movie-loving friends and assign each one a role from a movie you all know well.

Pop in a DVD but turn off the sound. As you watch the now-silent movie, everyone plays his or her part and speaks the words. For a funny twist, turn off the sound on a movie you've never seen before and provide your own dialogue as it plays!

# #52. STAGE a Play

If you've got the acting bug, try staging a play.

Write your own play or use an existing one. Your library should have a selection.

Cast your siblings and friends. Give them copies of the script. Hold rehearsals so your actors learn their lines, where to stand, and what to use for props. Your living room floor can be the stage.

Create programs listing each actor and her role. Invite your family and friends to opening night. Serve refreshments during intermission. The thing you want to hear at the end of that night is "Bravo!"

# #53. CALCULATE Your Worth

You don't have to crack open your piggy bank or withdraw all your savings. You're calculating the worth of your possessions, not your money.

Make a list of everything you own—books, toys, games, souvenirs, sports equipment, posters, etc. Most of it is probably in your room, but don't forget outdoor stuff like bikes and skis.

Estimate how much each item costs. If you don't know, look in the classified ads in the Sunday newspaper or go to an online shopping or auction site to see what price used things like yours go for. Use a calculator and add up the total. It's fun to see what it is, but it means nothing, really, assuming you want to keep your belongings.

# #54. Visit a MILITARY BASE

The United States has one of the largest armed forces in the world. Hundreds of military bases operate in America and many more overseas.

A permanent base is called an installation. Many bases or installations allow visitors, and some even arrange group sleepovers! Call a nearby base and ask if and when you can tour it. Check out this site: usmilitary.about.com/od/theorderlyroom/l/blstatefacts.htm for state-by-state lists of installations and their phone numbers.

As the officers at the base will tell you, and as you would expect, there are rules when visiting.

Those rules are called protocol. Protocol is a code of conduct in official situations. Don't by shy, though. If you are granted permission to come, your hosts will be happy to answer all your questions.

"At ease" is what a superior officer might tell a soldier when he or she wants the soldier to relax. Be "at ease" yourself, but also be courteous. Ask before taking photos or going anywhere. Remember that you're in a place where people are working and where security is very important.

# #55. DRAW a Still Life

Life can move pretty fast. One way to slow down for a while is to draw a still life—a group of objects that aren't going anywhere and won't rush you.

A still life is a drawing or painting of inanimate (nonliving, nonmoving) objects. First you'll need to gather together various objects that you'd like to draw. Sure, you can draw a bowl of fruit or a vase of flowers, but you can also create odder collections of things that don't normally go together. What about an old sneaker, a banana peel, and a pair of scissors? Or a teddy bear and a watermelon?

Take a sketch pad and a pencil and tackle your composition. As with any art, don't worry if it doesn't look right—there is no right or wrong in art. Try different arrangements, lighting, and backgrounds.

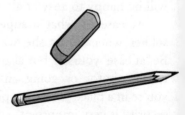

# #56. Make a MEAL for Your Family

What, you can't cook? Well, most kids can't, but it's just because they've never tried.

You'll need adult supervision, but you can prepare a healthful meal quite easily. Make sure everyone will be home on the night you cook, then plan your menu.

Here's an easy one: tossed salad, pasta with tomato sauce, and chilled fruit salad for dessert.

**SALAD:** Wash lettuce in cold water and tear into pieces. Add some sliced cucumbers, peeled carrots, tomatoes (making sure you wash all these first), and maybe some grated cheese. Toss in a bowl and serve with salad dressing.

**PASTA:** Boil water, add pasta, and cook for about ten minutes. Open a jar of tomato sauce, heat it up, and toss with cooked pasta.

**FRUIT SALAD:** Wash and slice a selection of fruits into little pieces, mix together in a bowl, and refrigerate until it's time for dessert.

Set the table, yell "Dinner!" and they'll come running. *Bon appétit!*

What goes on in those tall office buildings? What is happening in the back of restaurants? We all have wondered at one time or another how other people work and how certain businesses are run.

Make a list of stores, restaurants, or other companies in your community that you are curious about. With a parent's help, call or visit these places and ask if you could observe them for a few hours one afternoon. Be flexible and say you will be able to come whenever it is convenient for them.

If you can, try at least two types of businesses—for example, an office and a restaurant, or a store and a government facility (like the post office).

After you observe, write a thank-you letter right away to the person or people who hosted you. Offer them the chance to observe you in school one day!

# #58. CLIMB Indoors

Even if you don't have a mountain in your backyard, you can still get the thrill of mountain climbing, and you don't have to fly to Tibet or the Swiss Alps.

Indoor, artificial mountains are becoming popular in more and more gyms. They're also called climbing walls. Maybe you've seen one—they often look like rock, but they're actually made of plastic and fiberglass. Some of them even move, to make you feel as if you're climbing a craggy, oversized conveyor belt!

Call a nearby gym to see if they have a climbing wall and if they offer classes for kids. A good class teaches you the basics, including knot tying, climbing safety, and common commands. Be prepared—it is tough. But it's worth the view. And you probably won't be chased by mountain goats.

# #59. BUILD an UNDERWATER CITY

Rome was not built, nor did Atlantis sink, in a day. But you can both build and sink a city in less than twenty-four hours—and you won't even break a sweat or get your hair wet.

Fill a rectangular fish tank or a fishbowl with water. Actually any large, clear glass or plastic container will do. Line the bottom with pebbles or gravel for your ground. Be inventive. What can you use for grass? For concrete? Anything plastic works well, as does rust-proof metal.

Now add to your city—buildings, street lamps, cars, trees, and even people. You can make these things out of clay or small plastic blocks, or you can buy them at a dollhouse store, pet store, or toy store. Anchor the buildings and other objects in the gravel so that they don't float away. Voila! You've created an instant underwater city.

# #60. WRITE Yourself a Letter

Even if you have a hundred friends, you probably don't get many letters—written on real paper, at least.

You don't have to wait for your grandparents, or the kids you met at summer camp, to write to you.... Write a letter to yourself. Grab a piece of paper and a pen and write down whatever it is you're thinking, your favorite jokes, your happiest memories, or what you did today. The letter can be as long or as short as you want. You can illustrate it or include a photo or two.

Seal it in an envelope and address it, but don't mail it. Wait at least two months. If you can, wait a year. Then mail it. Or give it to your parents and ask them to mail it to you in ten years. When you're older, it will be like a blast from the past to get a letter from your younger self.

Do the hustle, dance the mashed potato, wriggle to the rumba—in other words, shake your body on the dance floor!

Every generation invents its own dances. The waltz and the polka were favorites in centuries past. The Charleston was popularized in the 1920s. Soon after, the fox-trot and the jitterbug swept the nation. The 1950s brought rock and roll and dances like the twist. Disco hit in the 1970s, and break dancing was a craze in the 1980s.

Ask your parents or grandparents to show you a few steps of their favorite dance. They may say they're a little rusty, but be enthusiastic and they'll start to remember!

You can also learn to dance by taking lessons. Or you can just turn on your favorite CD and move your body to the music whichever way you feel.

Humans have been dancing since prehistoric times, often in rituals and at celebrations. Your new dancing skills will come in handy at weddings and school dances. Besides, it's really fun, and pretty good exercise, too.

# #62. SURVEY Your Friends

Just about everybody has an opinion about something, but not everyone is willing to share that opinion. Some might be afraid that others will disagree with them.

A simple way to find out what people think about a certain subject without putting anyone on the spot is to take an anonymous survey. That way everyone can feel free to be completely honest.

Choose a hot topic to survey your friends, classmates, or neighbors about—for example, a recent scientific breakthrough, a new blockbuster film, or a popular Web site. Or you can survey a school issue, such as the quality of food in the school cafeteria, or the condition of the playground.

Write a simple questionnaire about the topic and hand out copies to your classmates or drop them in your neighbors' mailboxes (be sure to ask your teacher's or parents' permission first). Tell people not to put their names on the questionnaire. After a few days, collect the surveys and tally your results. Share your findings with your school or local paper.

# #63. CREATE a TRAVEL BROCHURE

Travel agencies display posters and brochures enticing people to visit exotic, faraway places. What if travel agencies in those faraway places displayed brochures enticing people to visit *your* town?

Create a travel brochure or poster that would make any person from those distant places fall in love with your town and immediately want to book a direct flight there. For inspiration, look at a brochure or two from one of the travel agencies.

Think about what makes your town special. Did a famous person grow up there? Did someone in your town invent something interesting or weird like the rubber band or the electric alarm clock? Do you have an especially beautiful park? Mention the things that people want most in a vacation: beautiful places, ways to relax, inexpensive attractions, and convenience. Find an angle that sounds exciting (as long as it's true!). History and trivia facts can also sell a place. Illustrate your brochure with colorful drawings and photographs.

# #64. PAINT the Sun

Twice a day our closest star puts on quite a show. It pokes up brightly in the morning, then slips behind the horizon with a brilliant splash in the evening. We usually ignore it. Pay attention next time!

But don't look yet—paint first. Paint what you think a sunrise or sunset looks like, then compare it to the real thing.

The newspaper and the local weather forecast usually give the exact rise and set times for your area, or you can check out www.almanac.com. With your painting in hand, watch the sunrise or sunset—or better yet, watch both in the same day.

Try to catch the sun coming up or setting every day for a week. You'll probably see different colors and patterns each time—crazily shaped streaks of all sorts of purples, reds, pinks, and more. One sunrise or sunset may look sort of like your painting, but not exactly....

**Make sure you look east for the sunrise and west for the sunset. Otherwise you'll be quite unimpressed!**

# #65. TELL a GHOST Story

Whether or not you believe in phantoms, apparitions, or specters, telling stories about them is a wild way to spend the night. On the next stormy night, invite your family or friends to a scare-fest. Sit in a circle and turn out the lights; then take turns telling the scariest, most bone-chilling stories you know. Pass a flashlight from storyteller to storyteller. Hold it under your chin so it shines on your face for a scary, distorted effect.

If you don't know any terrifying tales, prepare in advance by hunting for stories in books, on the Internet, or just asking around. Check your town's history. There might be a nearby inn that's rumored to be haunted, or perhaps there've been sightings of a mysterious white figure that walks your woods at night.

However, if checking with the locals is a dead end (so to speak), make up one of your own!

# #66. SAVE Turtles

Turtles have survived for millions of years. Now, because of human interference—in the form of coastal development, pollution, and hunting—turtles are being threatened with extinction. All it takes to save them is human awareness.

Learn about the threats to turtles in your area, and write an informed letter to the editor of a local newspaper and to state and federal government representatives who have a strong environmental platform.

The United States requires shrimp fishers to use Turtle Excluder Devices (TEDs) that allow turtles to escape nets so they don't drown. Be sure to eat only certified turtle-safe shrimp, which you can identify by a label on the packaging. If you buy shrimp at a fish market, ask if it is turtle-safe. Recycle plastics so they don't end up in the ocean where they entangle sea creatures. Don't release helium balloons—they often land in the ocean and can kill turtles if eaten.

Find out more online at www.seaturtles.org and other sites.

# #67. VOLUNTEER at a Soup Kitchen

Do you have some extra time on your hands? Volunteer at a soup kitchen, homeless shelter, or food bank.

Most communities have some type of food program for the needy and homeless, where volunteers are very welcome. It's kind of like being a waiter or waitress, except you won't get tipped.

In some soup kitchens, you'll be serving fresh, hot food to people as they walk along the "buffet table." Other times you'll be asked to bring plates of food to people at tables. Either way, you're giving warm nourishment to people who appreciate it more than they might be able to express.

> **Volunteering your time to make other people's lives better will help make the world a better place. Moreover, doing good is a surefire way to feel good yourself.**

# #68. FROLIC in a RAINSTORM

At the first sign of rain, most people run for cover, or at least for an umbrella. What's the matter? Do we think we are going to melt?

A little rain never hurt anyone. Show you're not afraid to get a little wet the next time a summer storm hits. As long as there is no lightning, the only things to fear from a summer shower are wrinkly fingers and toes.

Go crazy—run and dance. Get some friends and throw a ball around. Try doing things that you'd normally do in the sun—organize a basketball game, play tag, or throw a tea party.

The first few drops may be a shock, but soon you'll be soaked and it won't bother you a bit. If it's a hot day, you'll feel refreshed, but stay inside on cold rainy days— you could get chilled.

**At the first sign of lightning, go inside—never under a tree or near metal.**

# #69. BE a TOWN CRIER

Before the Internet, TV, or newspapers, people stayed informed thanks to town criers. These were citizens hired to walk through the streets, often in the evening, and shout out the day's events.

Today, most towns and cities are too big and noisy for town criers. Bring your neighborhood back a few hundred years and be a town crier for an evening.

Hand out flyers or send e-mails to your neighbors a few days in advance explaining that you are going to be a town crier for an evening. Let them know what day and time they can hear you. That day, listen to the local and national news and write out (or memorize) one- or two-line summaries of the top stories. Be sure to wear some reflective clothing if it's near dark. Walk down the street proclaiming the news for all to hear. If the houses are spaced far apart, repeat the news in front of every house.

You'll have an experience almost nobody else has had for about two hundred years.

# #70. ELIMINATE a Sense

Most humans have five senses: sight, hearing, taste, smell, and touch. Some people, such as those who are blind or deaf, have fewer.

Having senses is a gift, and experiencing the world without one, even temporarily, is a worthy challenge. Choose one sense to lose for an hour. The easiest ones to lose are sight (with a blindfold) and hearing (with earplugs). You can also block your sense of smell with nose plugs. Can you think of a way to eliminate your senses of taste and touch?

When you decide to eliminate a sense, make sure you bring along a friend (who is using all five senses). Do as many things as you'd normally do, but nothing that puts you in danger. Don't ride your bike while blindfolded, for example.

### Some activities to try:

- ◎ Make a snack.
- ◎ Watch TV (or listen, depending on the missing sense).
- ◎ Draw a picture.
- ◎ Clean your room.
- ◎ Go shopping.

# #71. ASK about an Older Person's DREAMS

We're not talking about the dreams you have while sleeping. Anybody at any age can have dreams about what they want to do in life.

When young people dream about the future, it's often about what job they want, where they want to live or travel, and even who they want to marry. Older people may have already had jobs and houses and husbands and wives, but they still have plenty to dream about.

If you don't believe it, ask them. Ask your grandparents or aunts or uncles, or any older people you know, what their dreams are about the future. Maybe they dream about having a second career or traveling to some far-off land or even running for political office.

You'll make someone happy by asking about his or her dreams (who doesn't like to talk about that?), and you'll see that no matter how old you get, there is always something to look forward to in life.

# #72. MAKE a Personality Collage

Words aren't the only way to express who you are and what you feel—you can express yourself with images, too.

Spend an afternoon with a stack of old magazines, a pair of scissors, some tape or glue, and a piece of cardboard. Search through the magazines to find bits and pieces of yourself—who you like, what you're interested in, how you feel.

Cut out anything you want, including photos, illustrations, words, or phrases. Look for words or phrases that describe your personality, like *adventure*, *dare to dream*, *one to watch*, or whatever else you feel says something about you. Collect the cutouts on the cardboard as you go. Once you have all the pieces you want, arrange them on the cardboard and glue them down.

Because this is an interpretive collage, don't include photos of yourself and your family. You want to give a feel for who you are, not a literal depiction.

# #73. BREAK a Piñata

Take a whack at a sweet Latin American custom—the piñata.

A piñata is a brightly decorated, hollow figure usually shaped like a bull or a donkey. Generally made of papier-mâché or clay, a piñata is stuffed with candy and hung from the ceiling for the sole purpose of being hit with a stick and broken.

Wait a minute—hit with a stick? Sounds violent, but it's actually a children's game that originated in Latin America.

The idea is to break the piñata open so the treats fall to the ground. The catch is that everyone who tries to hit the piñata is blindfolded. You are spun around a few times and sent roughly in the direction of the piñata. You get a few swipes, then you pass the stick to the next person. Regardless of who strikes the final blow, the goodies are for all to share.

You can make your own piñata out of papier-mâché (check out the Internet or a craft book for instructions), or you can buy one at most party-supply stores.

# #74. WRITE a Haiku

*Writing a haiku*
*Is not as difficult as*
*Some people believe.*

A haiku is a Japanese poem with three unrhymed lines. The first line has five syllables, the second has seven, and the last has five again. (Remember, syllables, not words.)

Haiku began gaining popularity in the fifteenth and sixteenth centuries and are still being written today. Traditionally, haiku are about nature, but don't limit yourself. You can write a haiku about anything you want.

It's a wonderful little surprise to write a personal haiku and post it on the fridge or put one in your parents' workbags so they'll find it later in the day.

Next time you're angry with a sibling, try expressing it in haiku:

*In the future, please*
*Don't borrow my books or toys*
*Without asking first.*

Don't be disappointed if you don't get a haiku apology back.

# #75. MAKE a Family Top Ten Countdown

We see lists everywhere we turn—magazine features, entertainment shows, refrigerator doors. Many of these lists are countdowns, keeping you hanging on till the end to see who or what claims that top spot.

Enjoy that feeling of anticipation in a whole new way. Create a top 10 countdown and present it to your family as it is done in showbiz—revealing one list item at a time, building to #1. You can do it by writing the countdown on a large piece of paper or poster board and covering each item with a strip of paper, or you can do it on the computer.

The countdown topic is up to you, but here are some possibilities to jumpstart your thinking:

◙ most embarrassing moments
◙ funniest vacation photos
◙ best Halloween costumes
◙ angriest mom and dad have been

You can even have your family guess as you go through the countdown. Whoever gets the most right must create the next top 10 list.

# #76. BUILD a Bat House

Only three species of bats are vampire bats, meaning they suck animal blood. Most bats eat insects instead. Before you get grossed out, remember that without bats, we would be dealing with an insect infestation—a single bat can eat about six hundred insects per hour!

For all the good bats do, it seems unfair that birds get all the nice houses. Let's change that!

A bat house can look similar to a birdhouse, and it's just as easy to make. Even if you don't live in an area where bats flap at night, you'll have fun building one.

For more information on bats and building a bat house, check out www.batconservation.org and www.batcon.org.

- ◎ Get six pieces of wood, each one about as big as the front of a large cereal box. With an adult's help, cut a bat-size hole in one of the pieces (the wall with the "door"). Nail or glue the four walls to the fifth piece, the floor, then attach the roof.
- ◎ Put it where the bats will find it—in an attic, a garage, a barn, or a tall tree—and hopefully a flying insect-eater will soon stop by.

# #77. DESIGN a Family Mascot

Mascots are characters created to generate spirit (at sport games or in schools) or sales (for companies).

Mascots are chosen because they say something about the company or team. For example, the Chicago Bulls basketball team wants to be thought of as strong like a bull.

Create a mascot for your family. What kind of animal or object exemplifies you? Are you all tall? Try the Giraffes. Are you quick? Try the Lightning. Once you decide on your mascot, draw a logo that incorporates it. You can even print it on T-shirts for everyone!

# #78. FIND a School Mascot

If your school doesn't have a mascot, hold a contest to produce one. The winning creation will be a part of your school's history!

Publicize the contest by posting flyers around school. Entries must include a drawing of the mascot and its name. Choose a group of teachers and students to pick a winner.

Ask your school to produce merchandise such as T-shirts or mouse pads that display the new mascot.

# #79. COMPILE Class Stats

Your class is probably pretty evenly split between girls and boys, and the kids in it are all about the same age. What about the statistics beyond that? The ones that are not obvious just by looking?

Make a list of facts that you would be interested to know about your classmates' lives outside the classroom. Poll your class and create a chart displaying the results. Here are some statistical questions you can ask:

- How many states has each student lived in? Does your class represent all fifty?
- How many countries has each student visited?
- How many siblings each student has—does your class have more than one hundred?
- How many bones has the class broken?
- How many languages does the class speak?

Come up with several other questions. You may discover that your class is made up of some interesting people!

# #80. MAKE a Map

Every day you probably follow the same route to get to school. Do you know it well enough to map it?

Whether you hop on a bus, take a subway, ride a bike, go by car, or walk to school, try to make a map of your school route from memory.

Go through the streets in your mind and transfer them to paper. If you get stuck, don't worry—you can look at another map, or retrace your path.

Now that you've got the cartography (mapmaking) bug, make a floor plan of your home. You may never have seen an architectural blueprint. Try to look at one before doing your plan. Check online or ask friends who have helped to build a new house.

New maps are made all the time because landscapes—both natural and human-made—change all the time. If you're interested in maps, read more about how they are made. Maybe a company that makes maps is close enough for you to visit and tour. Suggest it as a school field trip.

> **You can make the map topographic—include hills, mountains, streams, roads, and any other land feature.**

# #81. HELP Shovel Snow

You can't stop the snow from falling, but you can help shovel it.

After a snowstorm, put on a few layers of clothing under your outdoor winter clothes, wear warm gloves and boots, and grab your shovel. Walk through your neighborhood looking for sidewalks and driveways to clear.

When you see people who are already shoveling, offer to take over or lend a hand. The best candidates are older people and people who look exhausted. If you don't see anyone, you may approach people you know and ask if you can lend a hand, and a shovel.

It's a good idea to shovel the snow in front of your own house first. Your parents will definitely respect your generosity with others a lot more when their car isn't stuck in your snow-covered driveway.

**If snow is never in your forecast (hello, Florida), try coming up with a similar good deed that better suits your climate.**

# #82. SING A Cappella

One of the world's most beautiful musical instruments is not part of any orchestra—it's the human voice.

A cappella is an Italian phrase that means "in the style of a chapel choir." Basically it means singing without any accompanying instruments. Gather some of your music-loving friends and form an a cappella group.

Listen to a few a cappella songs to get the feel. Then decide on a song you'd like to experiment with. Most songs can be performed a cappella. As long as it has lyrics, the song can be any style—rock, country, rap, rhythm and blues, or whatever else you like. Practice the song as a group.

Now get a little inventive. Instead of having everyone sing the words, assign each person a musical instrument to try to duplicate with his or her voice. Someone with a deep voice can do the *boom bada boom* of the drums. If the song has *doo doo doo*s or *tra la la*s in the background, one person can do those while another person sings lead. Keep practicing the song until it sounds smooth.

# #83. LEARN Your Sign in Chinese Astrology

Next time someone calls you a snake, don't take it the wrong way. It might be because you were born in 2001.

In the Chinese calendar, every year is named after one of the following twelve animals: rat, ox, tiger, rabbit (hare), dragon, snake, horse, sheep (goat), monkey, rooster, dog, or pig. The cycle repeats every twelve years, starting again with the Year of the Rat.

There are multiple stories that explain the Chinese zodiac. According to one of those stories, Buddha (ca 563–483 BCE), the founder of Buddhism, once asked all animals to come to him, and only those twelve did, in that order. He rewarded them by naming a year after each.

Learn what qualities people born in your year are said to possess. Do some research online or at the library to find out which animal corresponds to the year you were born.

# #84. MAKE a Boomerang Note

Throw a boomerang—a curved, wooden weapon used by Australian aborigines—and it will come back to you. You can also throw a paper boomerang and see if that comes back.

Draw a big boomerang on a piece of paper. At the top of the page, write that this is a boomerang note that must reach at least twenty-five people before being returned to the thrower—you—by the end of that day. Everyone who receives the note must write his or her name and the time, and then pass it on. Once twenty-five people have signed it, the boomerang note can be returned…but it doesn't have to be, especially if it's not the end of the day. It's fun to see how many more people the note can reach.

Throw your boomerang note first thing in the morning at any gathering with more than twenty-five people. It's kind of like a chain letter, only it doesn't promise you good luck. But you might need a little luck to get it back.

# #85. SAVE an Endangered Animal

A species of animal or plant is considered endangered when it is close to extinction, or dying out. Diseases, predators, and humans can cause a species to be added to the list.

The first animal on the endangered species list was the peregrine falcon, in the late 1970s. California condors, California northern squirrels, gray bats, wood bison, American crocodiles, Florida manatees, giant pandas, mountain gorillas, red wolves, and tigers are only a few of the animals currently endangered. Are any of them in your neighborhood? Look into the local wildlife and find out what's in danger. You can do this by researching in the library, looking online, checking with the U.S. Fish and Wildlife Service in Washington, D.C., or contacting an animal rights group or a veterinarian. Raise awareness about your endangered neighbor by writing a letter to the local newspaper.

**Find out what else you can do to help endangered animals by visiting the World Wildlife Fund's Web site at www.worldwildlife.org.**

# #86. DRAW a Person at the Reverse Age

Did you ever hear people say about a cute baby, "He will be so handsome when he's older"?

If there are any babies in your family, think about how they might look as kids your age, teenagers, or even grown-ups. Try to draw them at one of those ages. Look at the baby in person or at a photograph of the baby.

You can do this with any baby you know, or even with a photo of a baby from a book or magazine. It will be more fun if you know the baby, though, because you can hold on to your drawing and compare it to the real thing in a few years!

You can try the reverse of this with an adult you know—draw him or her as a baby, or a kid your age. When you're done, ask the adult for a baby photo to see how close you were.

Another idea is to draw yourself much, much older. Don't leave out the wrinkles—you're only human!

# #87. CELEBRATE Your Town's Birthday

Your town probably wasn't born yesterday. Most likely it's been around for a while. Find out how long it has existed and how life has changed since it was founded.

Does your town have a welcome sign along the road where you enter it? If so, check it out. Most welcome signs say which year the town was founded. To find out more, head over to the local library or historical society, or even to your town's Web site. There you should be able to find plenty of information about what life was like before fast-food restaurants and oversize supermarkets dotted the landscape.

Take a walk to the town green or park. Many towns have memorials to people who have fought in wars or monuments to famous or important residents. Ask your grandparents or other older town residents what the town was like when they were young. Chances are, it's changed a lot since then.

You can even celebrate your town's birthday, if you can figure out where to send a card.

# #88. MAKE Going-Away Envelopes

Next time your parents or a good friend goes away, send them off with a little something to remember you by—every day.

The custom is that vacationers bring something back for you, not that you give them something when they leave. But there is always room for new customs.

For every day the person is going to be away, fill an envelope with a different surprise. Ask him or her to open one envelope every day. This gives your loved one something to look forward to, which is especially nice if it rains or a flight is delayed.

Put the envelopes in a small paper bag and give it to the person you'll miss when they leave.

> The envelopes can contain anything you think would bring about a smile—drawings, poems, magazine clippings, photos, or riddles. If you have a little money to spend (although you don't have to), you can buy inexpensive gifts like stickers, gum, or a bookmark—or useful items like a calling card, extra shoelaces, lip balm, or a pen.

# #89. INSTALL a Black Lightbulb

You've seen those black light bulbs. Spooky!

These special lightbulbs plunge everything into darkness except anything that's white—which is illuminated. Under a black light, everyone has shockingly whitish purple Cheshire cat teeth! And light clothing or objects also glow brightly.

A black light is made with dark blue glass and does not have the usual white coating that common bulbs do. It gives off ultraviolet radiation, which is absorbed by certain things (such as most white fabrics), making them appear to glow. This kind of radiation is not known to be dangerous.

Black lights are available in party stores and most hardware stores for a few dollars. Next time you have a party and want to make it shine, light it up with a black lightbulb.

# #90. CONVERT Your Allowance

How many British pounds do you get a week for allowance? How about Japanese yen? Or French francs, or Indian rupees?

If you get a weekly or monthly allowance, you're most likely paid in U.S. dollars (unless you live in a foreign country, of course!). In another country, your allowance may buy more or less than it could in America, depending on how much a dollar is worth in that country's currency (it varies from country to country).

To find out how much your allowance is worth in a foreign currency, go to a bank or currency exchange company. You can also look in the newspaper for exchange rates. Another way is to search online. Try The Universal Currency Converter at www.xe.net/ucc. Type in the dollar amount and select the type of money you want it converted to; the site will do the math.

If you don't get an allowance, choose any amount of money—like how much you paid for your latest DVD, or how much your favorite candy bar costs—and convert it to a foreign currency.

# #91. NAVIGATE the Woods

Hundreds of years ago, people had to navigate on land every day without the help of highways, street signs, or sometimes even maps. It was all wilderness, all the time.

Go for a hike in the woods and find your way using just a compass and a map. We rarely need to know which way is north—or east or west or south, for that matter. But it is easy to learn. All you need is a compass and the sun. A compass needle always points north, and the sun rises in the east and sets in the west.

Besides a compass and a map, take an adult who knows what he or she is doing in the woods (and where you are going).

### For any hiking trip, woods or otherwise, bring the following:

- ◎ layers of clothes (so you're prepared for hot or cold weather)
- ◎ a flashlight
- ◎ healthful food like granola and dried fruit
- ◎ water

# #92. REARRANGE Your Room

For as long as you can remember you've had your bed near the window, your desk against a wall, and your dresser against the other wall. Mix it up a little! There is no rule that says your room must remain the same for all time.

You can't make your room any bigger, but you can keep it interesting by doing a little redecorating. Try turning your bed around, having it stick out into the room, or moving it to the opposite wall. Put your desk in front of the window. Use a bookshelf as a room divider.

Switch your posters around, or put up new ones. Cut out pictures from your favorite magazines and tack them to the walls. You might want to take new photographs of your friends and family and hang them up, too.

This is a great time to get rid of anything you don't want or no longer use and donate it to charity. You'll have more room to experiment.

Be careful the next time you run into your room and jump on your bed. Make sure you remember where you moved it!

# #93. WRITE a Song Parody

Part of the price of popularity is parody. The more people like something, the more likely it is that someone will make fun of it.

You've probably heard songs that have been rewritten with joke lyrics. Radio stations do it sometimes, and so do some rock stars.

Take a song you really like, or one you really hate, and rewrite the lyrics into something funny, line by line. It's even more hilarious if you choose a song that most people know—popular songs on the radio, children's songs like "Twinkle, Twinkle, Little Star" and Christmas carols are all good targets. It helps to have the real lyrics written out.

Even though your song is a parody, make it about something, not just nonsense phrases. For example, if the song is called "Happy with You," you could turn that into "Stick It with Glue" or "Is That Your Shoe?"

When you are done, sing the completed version to family and friends, with the real song playing in the background. You're sure to get lots of laughs.

# #94. SPIN the Globe

School lessons are planned in advance, but there are more spontaneous ways to learn. For this one, you need only a globe or a map, your pointer finger, and your curiosity.

Close your eyes, spin the globe, and stop it with your finger (or close your eyes and then put your finger on the map). Write down the name of the country you pointed to. Do this four more times and write the country name each time. If you land on a place you know well—the United States, for example—pick again.

Once you have five countries, look each one up in an encyclopedia or online and find out everything you can about it—such as, what language is spoken, what the biggest cities are, how long it would take you to travel there, what people eat, and what kids your age do for fun.

# #95. MAKE a String Path

Some say that there is a pot of gold at the end of the rainbow. But what about at the end of a long piece of string?

Next time you give a gift, give it with a little mystery. Create a long string path leading your mom, dad, sibling, or friend to a special surprise.

Tape one end of a ball of string somewhere near your house's front door. Then unwind it all through the house. Go upstairs and downstairs, through rooms, over furniture, and so on. Keep the string loose and be careful not to damage anything or run the string too close to anything that generates heat.

Decide on an end point and cut the string. That's where you put the present.

At the front door, leave a note next to the string that says something like, "Follow this string for a special surprise!" When the gift recipient walks in, he or she will have the exciting task of retracing your steps along the string path to the next best thing to a pot of gold—your present.

# #96. CLEAN Up Nature

Every year it's the same old parties—birthdays, Halloween, Christmas, Hanukkah, etc. This year, start a new tradition: an annual nature cleanup party.

Invite a bunch of friends and family to help clean up a nearby park, beach, or forest. Which area you choose depends on which is closest or dirtiest. A few weeks before the cleanup, write a letter to the local newspaper or post a request for volunteers on your city or town Web site.

Pack lunches and head out for a very fun and very rewarding day full of chatting, laughing, and doing good. Bring garbage bags and ties, plastic gloves, and a healthy spirit. All you have to do is pick up the trash! (Your parents will wonder why they couldn't get you to do this in your room.)

Wear those gloves and be careful when picking up things that are sharp or dangerous. If you're unsure about what something is, ask an adult.

You'll be surprised how much garbage you can collect, and you'll feel good about the results.

# #97. BALANCE a Book

We walk around perfectly balancing our heads on our shoulders all the time, no matter what. Since our heads are attached, it's a piece of cake. But what if you had to walk around with a book balanced on your head?

Test your balance. Put a book (not a huge encyclopedia—just an average-size novel) atop your noggin and walk as far as you can around the house with it. If you can make it more than a few feet without dropping the book, step it up a notch. Go up or down some stairs with the book. And if you can do that, you could try playing tennis or surfing with the book on your head, but that might be taking this balancing act one step too far.

In order to keep the book up there, your back and neck must be perfectly straight. This will surely improve your posture, which will keep your parents from saying, "Sit up straight!"

# #98. TAKE Illusion Photographs

You can't hold the White House or the Eiffel Tower in your hand, but make it look like you can.

Illusions are everywhere, but some don't appear unless you arrange them.

Choose an object that is way too big to hold, such as a house, a statue, a car, or even a person. Stand in front of it and hold your hand out to the side, like a waiter carrying food. Have a friend look at the scene through a camera and tell you how far in front of the object you have to stand so that it looks small compared to you, small enough to hold. If it's really big, you'll have to be pretty far away for this to work.

When you're at the right distance, your friend may have to crouch, bend, or somehow position himself or herself with the camera so that it looks like you're holding that big object in your small hand.

When the view is perfect and the illusion is created, your friend snaps the photo. You're an instant giant!

# #99. LIST Your Firsts

Even though your life has been pretty short so far, you've already accomplished a lot—and you should be proud.

Go ahead and toot your own horn. Make a list of all your personal firsts. You can start with these, and then add on new firsts as you accomplish more.

- ◙ first word
- ◙ first step (day and location)
- ◙ first solid food
- ◙ first hobby
- ◙ first Halloween costume
- ◙ first pet
- ◙ first day of school
- ◙ first teacher
- ◙ first thing you wanted to be when you were older
- ◙ first friend
- ◙ first fear
- ◙ first trip (airplane, boat, train)
- ◙ first lesson (piano, karate, art, swimming, anything!)
- ◙ first injury (knock on wood!)

If you deface a dollar bill, you could be fined one hundred dollars as punishment. You don't have to be a mathematician to know that that doesn't pay!

Defacing a dollar doesn't just mean cutting out George Washington's mug. It includes any disrespectful act—writing on it, ripping it, gluing it, or getting it dirty. There are lots of defaced bills out there. If you have one in your wallet, you can turn it in at a bank for currency that's in better shape. Even a bill that is merely worn out from excessive use may be exchanged.

Don't worry—the bank won't think you defaced the money. Since you're only trying to help a beat-up bill, they'll know you're an honest person.

If money is seriously damaged (by fire, water, chemicals, pests, or dirt), the Department of the Treasury, Bureau of Engraving and Printing, should replace it free of charge, but you have to mail it to them in Washington, D.C., in a special way. For full details, check out www.moneyfactory.gov/section.cfm/8/39.

# #101. PAINT with Nature

Store-bought paints are bright, convenient, diverse . . . and store-bought. Long before man-made paints, nature provided the benefit of color, and you didn't need to keep a receipt for returns. You still don't, if you paint with nature.

What qualifies as paint from nature is up to you. Try squeezing juice from berries, rubbing leaves or flowers, or smearing mud on a page. Tree bark and sticks can create marks, too. Take a sketch pad to a forest or field and experiment.

However, to be safe, check with a science teacher and an employee at a nursery before you go so that you know what to look for in your area—and what to avoid. Even if poison ivy makes a pretty green smear, you don't want to sacrifice your safety and comfort for your art. And even if your neighbor has dozens of the prettiest yellow daffodils in her yard, you have to ask before plucking.

> Art made from nature makes a wonderful gift, especially for Mother's Day and Father's Day. (Most dads still prefer store-bought rather than nature-painted ties, however.)

# #102. MAKE Anagrams

When is a horse a shore? When you're making anagrams.

An anagram is a word whose letters are rearranged to spell another word without adding or removing any letters and using each one once. Notice that both *horse* and *shore* have an *e*, an *h*, an *o*, an *r*, and an *s*. The two words are just a jumble away from each other.

Here are a few more:

rob—orb
plum—lump
crate—react (or trace)

You can also turn a word into an anagram phrase, or mix up the letters of a phrase to create an entirely different phrase. The phrases don't always make sense, though. For example, *splinter* can be *rent lips*. It's nonsense, but it's an anagram.

Make a few anagrams yourself. Start with three-letter words, then try some four-letter words. Next, try to make an anagram of your name. If your first name doesn't have an anagram, add your last name, too. Come on, give it a hots—um, shot.

# #103. RUN a PENNY Drive

A penny saved is a penny worth donating. Organize a penny drive to raise money for a good cause.

Get an empty, unusual container such as an old suitcase, a fish tank, or even a kiddie pool. Ask your school or library if you can place the container near the entrance with a sign explaining your cause. Announce the drive on your town's Web site, on flyers you post around town, and in the local newspaper.

When your drive is done, exchange the pennies for bills at the bank, and present the money to your favorite charity.

# #104. RUN a CLOTHING Drive

You can give to charities without having any money at all. Simply clean out your closet!

Round up clothes that you don't wear anymore and donate them to a homeless shelter or the Salvation Army.

Encourage your family and friends to do the same. Suggest that your school make a clothing drive an annual event. Set up boxes labeled by type of clothing, such as coats or shoes, in the school lobby.

# #105. FIND the Meaning of Your Name

Andrew means "courageous." Sarah means "princess." Kevin means "handsome." Bethany means "house of figs."

Most parents don't choose a name for a child because of what it means. Usually they like the way a name sounds, or they name the baby after a family member or friend. Regardless of why your parents gave you your name, find out what it meant when it was created, and where in the world it came from.

Books and Web sites that translate names are common and easy to find. Spend an afternoon with friends at a bookstore, in the library, or online checking one another's names. Try to define the names of your siblings, your parents, and other people you know as well.

On a big sheet of paper, make two columns: a list of the names of the kids in your class on the left, and a list of the meanings of those names (mixed up) on the right. Play a game in which people have to match the name with the meaning.

# #106. HOST a Formal Dinner

Wearing a jacket and a bow tie or a long dress and shiny shoes may not always be comfortable, but you have to admit that when you do, you look *marvelous*.

Don't wait for a holiday or a wedding to wear your nicest, fanciest clothes. Get dressed up on a regular, humdrum weekday. Suggest to your family having a formal dinner—ties and jackets for the gentlemen, dresses for the ladies. (That's actually semiformal— formal would be tuxedos and gowns.)

You won't have to do anything else differently. You don't have to buy expensive furniture or hire a string quartet to play quiet music while you eat. The food can be what you usually have for dinner, but you'll just eat it in style.

It will give everyone something special to look forward to during the week. And it's very possible that the change of pace will put everyone in a good mood, which will improve conversation—and maybe even the taste of your parents' cooking!

# #107. RACE the States

No, you will not be running from Maine to Alaska. (On second thought, exercise is good, so don't let us stop you!)

Rather, gather a friend or two or fifty and see who will be the first to list all fifty states on a piece of paper. You may think this sounds easy, but it can be tough even for geography buffs.

Because of that, all racers may take one minute before the contest begins to look at a list of the states. One minute may even be enough time to come up with a system for remembering—one second per state, plus ten more seconds for extra speed-cramming.

Surprisingly, people sometimes forget what might be considered some of the more obvious states, like New York or California. Few leave out their own state, but it sure would be funny if you did.

To add to the challenge, you can set a time limit. Whoever recalls the most states in, say, three minutes, is state-certified.

# #108. MEET Your Mayor

If the president is not returning your calls, try seeking out an elected official a little closer to home: your town's mayor.

Write a letter or make a phone call to the mayor's office and request a meeting. If the mayor doesn't have enough time to meet with you individually, ask your teacher to arrange a class field trip so that the entire class can meet the mayor. Or find out from the mayor's office if he or she is making any public appearances or holding any press conferences that you can attend.

Before your meeting, read up on local politics and prepare a few questions. You can also ask the mayor how he or she got started in politics and whether or not he or she plans to run for higher office (for state legislature, or even U.S. Congress). If you have any suggestions about changes or improvements that you'd like to see around town, now's your chance to bend the mayor's ear.

# #109. LEARN Your Bones

Four inside the ear. Thirteen in the wrist. Two in your big toe. All in all, you've got 206 of them in your body.

We're talking about your bones. Without them you'd be a shapeless pile of mush. When you were born, you had about four hundred bones in your skeleton. Take it easy, you didn't lose any—as you grew, many of your soft baby bones fused together into harder bones.

Now that you're older and your skull is a little bit more firmly in place, take it over to the library and fill it with facts about the thing that holds you together—your skeleton.

Using a good science book, trace the human skeleton and label the individual bones.

### Here are a few bone facts to whet your appetite:

◎ The clavicle, or collarbone, is the most frequently broken bone.

◎ The only bone that does not touch another is the hyoid, in the throat. It holds your tongue in place.

◎ The smallest bones are inside the ear.

# #110. COPY a Masterpiece

No artist could truly duplicate Leonardo da Vinci's great masterpiece the Mona Lisa, but that hasn't stopped people from trying.

Many artists have honed their skills by copying great works of the past and perfecting the techniques of the masters. As long as artists don't pass off their fakes as the real thing, there is nothing wrong with it. After all, imitation is the sincerest form of flattery.

Just like art students do, copy a masterpiece. Take your sketch pad and go to an art museum. Since most museums don't allow ink pens, bring a pencil or a piece of charcoal instead. Find a painting or sculpture that appeals to you. Then take your time and do several sketches of the work.

If your drawings don't look exactly like the original, don't worry. That's what practicing is all about.

Invite a group of the biggest liars you know over to your house and try catching them at their game. Become a human lie detector!

Ask each of your friends to make a list of ten statements about his or her life. Some of them must be true and some must be false. Have each person read his or her list out loud.

Watch them very carefully as they read, and determine if the statements are true or false based on the person's facial expression or body language. Try to picture how you act when you tell a lie. Do you get nervous, fidget, blush, look down, or even giggle? These are common signs that someone might be lying.

Body language reveals a lot about us, but it's not foolproof. Polygraphs (lie detectors), often used in criminal investigations, monitor a person's blood pressure, pulse, and respiration because those functions can change when people lie. However, even polygraphs are not always accurate because those functions do not always change when a person lies.

# #112. Be a MIME

The word *mime* comes from *pantomime*, which means "the technique of telling a story without using words." Mimes use facial expressions and body movements to act out a situation without speaking or using props.

Have you ever seen a mime pretend to be trapped in a box? The mime will feel all around himself or herself with flat palms as if he or she were touching the walls of a box and looking for a way out. Try it right now. Look in the mirror and ask someone to watch you and give you some feedback. Determine how big the box is so that you can feel your way around it in a more believable manner. Act out a few more things in mime and see if friends or family can guess what you're doing.

### Some mime actions to try:

◎ walking a dog
◎ washing dishes
◎ opening a can of soup
◎ lifting a heavy barbell
◎ dropping something and picking it up
◎ walking through a cobweb

# #113. PUBLISH a Family Newspaper

Honest reporting is hard work, but when it comes to your family, the whole truth must be told.

Keep your loved ones informed about what is happening with your family—publish a family newspaper. You don't have to limit your news to what's going on with people in your house—include grandparents, cousins, aunts, and uncles, too. Keep a list of stories that you'd like to share with the family. Any new babies born? Did anyone get an award at school or a promotion at work? Is anybody moving? Include photographs, jokes, and even a comic strip.

Think of a title that may include words such as *journal, courier, times, herald, globe,* or *post*—for example, *The Jones Journal* or *The Thomas Times.*

You can create the newspaper on a computer or with a pair of scissors and some glue. Either way, make copies of your finished product and send them to your entire family.

# #114. TRY New Foods

Take your taste buds on a worldwide voyage by sampling food from other countries.

You can partake of pad thai (Thailand), sample sushi (Japan), reach for risotto (Italy), and so much more. There is a world of dishes out there. Go to the international foods section of your grocery store and check out the variety. Look in the yellow pages under restaurants and invite your family to try something new—and foreign. Look for restaurants that serve cuisine from some of these countries: Japan, China, Ethiopia, Korea, El Salvador, Brazil, Italy, India, or Spain—just to name a few.

If you know people from another country, suggest a meal swap. You visit their house for an authentic dinner from their country, then you invite them over for an old-fashioned American meal, or whatever your family usually eats for dinner.

# #115. Walk for a CAUSE

Your brain is not the only part of your body with moneymaking potential. Your feet can earn money, too.

Pound the pavement for your favorite charity and take part in a walkathon. Many different groups sponsor annual walkathons to raise money and awareness for their cause. Registration pamphlets for some of them are often available at school, the post office, cafés, or stores. When you participate in a walkathon, you raise money by asking people to donate a certain amount based on how far you walk. If someone sponsors you two dollars for every mile you walk, for example, and you walk five miles, then you've raised ten dollars.

If someone in your family or in a friend's family suffers from a certain illness, you can join a walkathon to raise money to find a cure. No matter what cause you walk for, you'll be doing something you'll feel great about.

# #116. ENTER a Contest

Everybody is good at something. What's your talent? Enter a contest to see how you measure up to others who share your skills.

Whether it's pie eating, poetry writing, storytelling, spelling, or three-legged racing, there's a contest out there for every talent or interest. Find a contest that fits your interest and give it a go! Your school or town newspaper may announce contests sponsored by local or national organizations, and you can find others on the Internet. Before you enter, make sure you read all of the rules. That way you won't forget some small detail that could disqualify you.

Sure, we all want to win contests, but it's thrilling just to enter. If you enter the contest just for the fun of it, you won't be disappointed if you lose. And if you win, you'll be totally surprised.

Some contests may be judged subjectively—meaning that the judges choose winners based on how they feel at the moment. Don't get discouraged if you don't win. Keep trying—next year the judges may be in your favor.

# #117. PERSONALIZE Your Calendar

Why spend the year with pictures of people you don't know? Make a calendar using photographs of yourself and your friends or family.

You can either convert an existing calendar or create a new one from scratch. If you are converting a calendar, cut out twelve pieces of paper the same size as your calendar pages. Paste your photos on the paper, and then paste the papers into the calendar, right over the pictures that are already there.

If you're starting from scratch, you'll need thirteen pieces of stiff paper (construction paper or paperboard). With a hole punch, punch four evenly spaced holes along the top of each sheet. Bind the calendar by threading yarn or string through the holes and tying it. Flip up the first page and paste a picture on the top page. On the bottom page, either draw a calendar grid and fill in the days, or use a photocopy of that month's calendar page from an existing calendar. Repeat for every month.

Then fill up the calendar with social events!

# #118. Go THUMBLESS

Our thumbs really help us get through the day. We use them to grasp pencils firmly, hold toothbrushes, turn doorknobs, pull up zippers, hold a fork, pick up a glass, move a computer mouse, and much, much more. That's a lot of pressure!

Tape each thumb to your pointer finger or to your hand and try to get through an entire day without using your thumbs. Do everything that you normally do each day—write with a pencil, eat with a fork, brush your hair. You'll soon discover how important your thumbs are. You might feel very strange and wobbly as you write, and you may just create a huge mess trying to eat, but don't worry, it's all part of the adventure.

Humans are adaptable and always have been. If you had to, you could get used to doing things without thumbs. Even after five minutes without yours, you probably adjusted and were able to pick up certain things without much trouble.

# #119. CREATE Your Own Instrument

Many instruments, usually including strings, woodwinds, brasses, and percussion, are played in a symphony, but there's always room for one more.

Create a brand-new, never-before-seen instrument out of everyday household objects. Your instrument doesn't have to resemble anything that exists now in the orchestra, and it doesn't have to produce a familiar sound. Imagine how strange the bagpipes may have seemed when they were first heard and seen.

Some materials you can use to create your instrument include rubber bands, empty soda cans, cardboard boxes, and paper clips—anything that you think will make an interesting sound. Instruments are played in many ways, from banging on a drum to blowing into a flute. How will you play your instrument? By banging? Strumming? Tapping? Experiment until you find a sound you like.

# #120. Paint a MURAL

Murals are large paintings that cover an entire wall or side of a building. Show how proud you are of your town, school, or club—"mem-mural-ize" it in a mural.

With friends, choose a few sites where you think a mural would look great, like a local business, an apartment building, a children's museum, an old barn, a library, or your own school. Then prepare a pitch to ask for permission.

Come up with a positive theme that you'd like to mem-mural-ize. Multiculturalism, education, town history, or school spirit are just a few ideas. Sketch out two or three possible designs for the mural. The stronger the design, the more likely that you'll get it approved. So make it irresistible!

When your mural is approved, you can hold a fundraiser to buy the paints and brushes, but the painters—you and your friends—will work for free!

After you've finished painting, be sure to sign and date the mural and take a photo to commemorate its completion.

# #121. DESIGN Prank Packaging

Your sibling goes to the fridge and takes out the milk carton ... only it's not cow's milk. It's rat milk?!?

Choose a household item and design a prank label for it. Computer skills are required—at least if you want half a chance of actually fooling anybody. To create the most authentic-looking phony label you can, mimic the font and overall look of the real label while inserting some kind of joke.

When done, print it and use tape to carefully affix it to the product package. You will probably have the best luck if you use a product that already has a paper label, such as bottled water or canned pasta. That way, the feel of paper won't tip off your prank victim right away.

You can also redo just a portion of the label— for example, you can change only the name or the ingredients of a product. Turn *Raisin Bran* into *Raisin Barf* or *cottage cheese* into *rotted cheese*.

Just be sure you're there when someone discovers the prank. Making prank labels is fun, but watching other people's reactions is usually even more fun.

# #122. RUN a GESTURE Spelling Bee

Run this bee as any other—participants take turns trying to spell the given word. However, they will not be spelling out loud—they will write the word in the air! This means the moderator must "read" the gesture to get the word. Speller and moderator should face the same direction so the moderator can "read" the speller's word properly. Spellers should "write" slowly and use all capital letters.

Once the speller air-spells the word, both he and the moderator write it down—the speller the way he spelled it, the moderator the way he read it.

◉ If the speller and the moderator both get the word right, the speller stays in the bee.

◉ If the speller spells the word right and the moderator reads it wrong, the speller stays in and gets to skip a turn (meaning he has one less chance of being eliminated).

◉ If the speller spells the word wrong and the moderator reads it right, the speller is out.

◉ If the speller and the moderator both get the word wrong, the speller stays in the bee.

# #123. BUILD a Birdbath

Make a birdbath for your feathered friends and watch them flock to your yard.

If you want to attract birds to your lawn, it helps if you give them a reason to come. Birds always need water to drink (especially in the summer) and to bathe in. If you set out a birdbath, your yard could become the hangout for your winged neighbors.

The birdbath doesn't need to be anything fancy. Find a large ceramic bowl or basin that your family no longer uses (better check with your parents first). Prop the bowl up on a few bricks or pieces of wood and keep it filled with about 2 inches of clean water.

Don't put your birdbath on the picnic table or the lawn furniture—unless you like bird poop, that is.

# #124. SERVE Breakfast in Bed

Surprise someone in your family with breakfast in bed. If you do it on a regular day (not on a birthday or Mother's Day or Father's Day, for example), they'll never see it coming!

On the day of the surprise, set your alarm early—before your special person gets up. The point is to wake the person up as you enter the bedroom with breakfast. Tiptoe into the kitchen and quietly prepare the meal. It doesn't have to be fancy—toast and OJ, a bagel, even a bowl of the person's favorite cereal.

Place everything on a tray and don't forget utensils, napkins, and a flower. Presentation is everything, and even cornflakes can appear elegant with the right touch.

Bring the breakfast to your special person and watch his or her surprised smile.

# #125. Run a CAR WASH

A great way to earn money and beat the heat is to wash cars. You can go into business for yourself or organize a group, such as your school, house of worship, or youth center, to raise money for a cause.

You won't need to buy a huge, mechanized car-wash system with all those spinning brushes and conveyor belts. Some soap, a hose, a few buckets, sponges, and elbow grease are all you'll need.

Run your car wash on a Saturday morning—that's when most people have time. Spread the word about your upcoming car wash by advertising in the local paper, posting a notice on your town's Web site, and sending e-mails to your friends and neighbors. Also, make posters and flyers and hang them around town.

First be sure to roll up the car windows!

# #126. LEARN a New Word

When someone calls you pulchritudinous, the proper response isn't "How dare you call me that?" You should simply say, "Thanks!" (It means "beautiful.")

There are thousands and thousands of words in the English language. There's no way anyone could know them all, but there's always room for a few more entries in our vocabularies. Add a few more words to your verbal repertoire every day for a week. To find words to learn, you can open the dictionary to a random page and choose a word you've never heard before. Or you can read a newspaper article or a difficult book and look up any word you don't know.

Once you've learned a new word, use it! (If you don't, chances are you'll forget it.)

You might have such a jocund (fun) time with your new words that you'll decide to learn a word a day for the rest of your life.

# #127. Kick a BAD HABIT

Do you bite your nails? Chew gum too loudly? Interrupt people all the time? Give those bad habits the boot.

Try a little self-motivation. Don't try to quit your bad habit because your mom or dad or teachers want you to. Do it because *you* want to!

Pick one habit you want to do away with. Promise yourself that for one hour you will not, under any circumstances, repeat that habit. Once you've mastered that for a few days, keep yourself from indulging in your habit for an afternoon, then graduate to an entire day. Then repeat—until you can go for two days in a row. Then three. And so on.

If you are having difficulty, try to think of something else that you can do whenever you get that bad-habit urge. For instance, whenever you feel like interrupting someone, count to ten to yourself first. Keep a calendar by your bed so that you can give yourself a star for that day if you didn't do your bad habit.

Once you've kicked your habit for a whole week, reward yourself for a job well done!

# #128. REPAIR a Stuffed Animal

Furry friends, both real and stuffed, get a lot of affection. The real ones can handle it, but the stuffed ones may begin to show wear and tear from so much love.

You probably have an old stuffed animal that has lost an eye, has a ripped leg, or had something else traumatic happen to it. Although those little wounds are love signs, you can repair them. It might make you both feel better.

You can take your stuffed friend to a tailor—some are stuffed-animal specialists—or you can repair it yourself with a needle and thread. Replacing a button or mending a small tear isn't very difficult. Ask your parents if they'll give you a quick course in Sewing 101.

If you can't find a missing eye or button, you can find replacements at a craft or sewing store. You might be able to get some mending tips there, too.

# #129. DISAGREE with an Adult

Young people once were not encouraged to have minds of their own. Adults finally realized that kids have something to say—even if it isn't always what the adults want to hear.

Disagree only when you have information to back up your opinion. State your reasons clearly and calmly for disagreeing. Listen to the other person's response and think before you answer. Disagreements can quickly turn into fights if both parties don't listen to each other.

# #130. ARGUE Someone Else's View

It's easy to argue your own opinion. But try arguing the opposite point of view.

For instance, you might think that you should be allowed to come home whenever you feel like it. But try to argue the issue from your parents' side. Why would they feel you need a curfew? (They're worried about your safety, for example.)

Looking at an issue from the opposite side might not change your mind, but it will remind you that most issues can have more than one answer.

# #131. CREATE an Animal Dance

Do you ever feel like prancing like a deer, hopping like a frog, slithering like a snake, scurrying like a squirrel, or waddling like a duck? Channel that creative energy into art, and choreograph an animal dance.

The animal world is full of graceful, goofy, bizarre, and amazing animal movements. Combine them into a zoological dance routine. For inspiration, watch a few nature shows or videos. Has anyone ever said that you look or act like a certain animal? If so, incorporate that animal's gait or giddiness into your dance. Use movements from as many animals as you'd like. Once your dance is finished, put on a recital and ask a family member or friend to videotape you as you perform.

In the last century, animals have influenced the movements (or at least the names) of lots of popular dances, such as the fox-trot, the pony, the jitterbug, the bunny hop, the fish, and the funky chicken. That leaves a lot of animals, from aardvarks to zebras, with no dance yet named in their honor.

The first American postage stamps were sold in 1847. Benjamin Franklin was on the five-cent stamp; George Washington was on the ten-cent stamp.

But what's on the latest hip postage stamp? Well, that's up to you.

Design a stamp featuring any person, place, or thing that you think deserves to be honored. Check out some of the existing stamps at the post office as well as the ones on the mail coming to your house. There are books and other resources that provide information on who has been on past stamps and how decisions are made about what to put on stamps. Do a little stamp-history research. It might spark an idea for your design.

Sometimes the post office asks the public to help them choose the next stamp image. Ask the post office if any selections are under way so that you can cast your vote.

Don't strain your eyes trying to make the stamp design actual size. Draw it any size you want. They have people who shrink these things.

# #133. Go to a DRIVE-IN Movie

Watch the latest Hollywood blockbuster from the comfort of your very own car—see it at a drive-in movie.

In 1933, the first drive-in movie theater opened in Camden, New Jersey. Drive-ins rapidly became quite the rage. People loved the novelty of watching movies outside in the privacy of their own cars. By 1958, there were over four thousand drive-in movie theaters across America.

Today, there are fewer than five hundred. You can find them, but you may have to look a little harder and drive a little farther to get to one. It's worth it.

Check the library for books on this charming trend of yesteryear, and visit www.driveintheater.com for a list of drive-ins still in operation.

On a nice summer evening, pile into the car and watch the stars under the stars.

# #134. GO Canoeing

Visit a lake or a river and spend a day paddling around in a canoe. The first canoes were hollowed-out tree trunks, but today most canoes are made out of fiberglass, plastic, or aluminum.

If you're new to canoes, you'll need a good teacher. Near lake resorts and larger rivers, you can usually find a company that rents canoes and offers lessons, too.

Some of the basics of canoeing are to stay balanced and not to lunge forward when paddling. But there's quite a lot more to it than that, and much of it you'll learn only by doing. You could read ten books on canoeing, but you have to get in the boat to get the feel of it.

No matter how skillful you become at canoeing, wear a life vest every time. It goes with a canoe the way a seat belt goes with a car.

# #135. TELL Stories in the ROUND

Get a bunch of people together and write stories. None of the authors will know how the stories end—they won't even know what the next lines will be.

Ask your writers to sit in a circle, notebook and pen in hand. For two minutes, everyone writes an opening paragraph to a story in his or her notebook. At the end of two minutes, everyone passes the notebooks to the right. Each author then continues the story for another two minutes. Keep passing the notebooks until everyone has written in everyone else's notebook.

Now ask each person to read the story in his or her notebook. You'll be amazed at how different (and funny) the stories turn out to be.

You can do the same thing with poetry, too. Have a different person write each line of a poem.

# #136. BE a TUTOR

Mention the word *tutor* to kids, and they usually think of *being* tutored. But kids can also be tutors themselves.

Find out if your school has a tutoring program and volunteer to help out. If not, let your teachers and guidance counselor know that you are available to tutor any students—those who are struggling or those who just need a little extra help.

You can also ask if your local library has a student tutoring program. Many libraries have after-school learning sessions for kids, as well as literacy, or reading, programs. They are always looking for volunteers.

You don't have to tutor people only in school subjects. You can teach other kids any skill or talent you possess—dancing, sports, music, crafts, or art. As a tutor, you'll find you're not only teaching but learning as well. You will gain a whole new appreciation for what your teachers do every day.

# #137. FIND Your DREAM JOB

What's it really like to be an astronaut and orbit the Earth in a space shuttle? Or to be a zookeeper and work with wild animals? Ask and find out!

Investigate just what it takes to have the job that you've always dreamed about. Make a list of three different occupations you'd love to have when you get older. Have you always wanted to be a lawyer or a doctor? What about a puppeteer or a clown?

Ask your parents or your teachers if they know anyone who holds the job you're dreaming of. Check the Internet, too. Lots of companies and organizations have Web sites where you can send e-mail to their employees.

Once you've found these special jobholders, ask them what it's like to do what they do. What is a typical day like? What kind of education or training did they need? Ask them for any advice they might have for someone your age who'd someday like to do what they do.

You'll get the real facts about your dream job, and they'll be flattered that someone wants to follow in their footsteps.

# #138. PLAY Animal Charades

Humans are no strangers to being called animals. If your room is messy, you may be called a pig.

Do something that is *really* wild—play animal charades. Now if you're called a pig, at least it will be based on your talents, not your messy ways! With friends or family, take turns acting out different animals for the others to guess. If you crave competition, form teams so that every charade becomes a race to see which team can figure it out first.

Write the names of many different animals on slips of paper before playing. Fold the slips and put them in a hat or bowl. Each player picks a slip and acts out that animal.

Be as specific as possible. For example, if the animal is a bird, all you'd have to do is flap your arms, and people would get the right answer. Go for the extra challenge and write "eagle." When acting that out, simply flapping your arms won't be enough. Think of other clues that will help convey "eagle"—America's national bird, bald head, back of a quarter, top of a flagpole!

# #139. TEST Weather Predictions

We can use perpetual calendars to tell us what day of the week November 28, 2012, or May 1, 3987, will fall on, but we can't say for sure if it will be sunny this weekend. That hasn't stopped us from trying to predict the weather.

In 1792, Robert Bailey Thomas began publishing an annual book that included long-range weather forecasts. It was named *The Farmer's Almanac*, renamed *The Old Farmer's Almanac* in 1848, and is still published today! Get a copy of *The Old Farmer's Almanac*. It comes out every September and is available at bookstores and newsstands. Use the almanac to test how accurate its predictions are. Did it predict a dry summer, but the weather was very rainy? Did it predict a cold winter, but it turned out to be unseasonably warm?

For a week straight, compare the almanac's predictions to nature's payoff. How accurate is it? More, or less, accurate than the groundhog on February 2? You can also find weather predictions region by region at www.almanac.com.

# #140. BECOME a Statue

Medusa, a character from Greek mythology, could turn people into stone just by looking at them. That's *one* way to become a statue. The hard way.

An easier way is simply to stand still, completely motionless, as if you were made of stone.

Turn yourself (and maybe a few friends, too) into stone and pretend to be a statue for an hour or so. You can pose like a famous statue that you've seen before, or you can create your own poses.

Freeze yourself on your front lawn or in a public park and see how many people walking or driving by are fooled! Remember, no matter how much people try to get you to move, do your best not to.

# #141. POSE for an Artist

We've all been to museums as visitors. Here's a way to (maybe) go to a museum—and stay there—as part of an exhibit.

Artists need human subjects to draw, paint, and sculpt. Sometimes they refer to memory or photographs, but they often create their masterpieces with a live person sitting right there in front of them. That can be you.

If there's an art school in your community, call and ask if they need any kid models. Maybe you know an artist who'd like to use you. You can also go to an art store and ask them if they have any ideas.

Sometimes artists who are studying anatomy need nude models—*not* the kind of posing you want to do. When you talk to the art school, make sure they know that you're a kid and that you'd be a clothed model.

Find the right artist and one day you could be immortalized on a museum wall.

# #142. FIND a Sister School

Right now there are millions of kids your age across the country and across the globe going to school, just like you. Reach out and find out what their lives are like.

Ask your teacher to help you find a sister school, either in the United States or in a foreign country. Maybe you can find a school with the same name as yours in another state. If you have a foreign exchange student in your class, perhaps you can get in touch with his or her school back home. You and your classmates could share stories, letters, and ideas with kids in Korea or Kansas, teens in Timbuktu or Tennessee, and children in Chile or Charleston—or anywhere else!

Pick a school in a town or city in a foreign country or a faraway state. Write a letter to that school (to the principal's attention) asking if they'd like to be your sister school. Then wait and see who responds!

# #143. KEEP a Phone Log

Do you make a lot of phone calls? Do you ever forget to call someone back, or forget who called you, and when?

Keep track in a phone log. Many businesses use them because they have to pay bills and must know exactly how they're spending their money. You can do it for fun, to see patterns, and to help remember things.

In a notebook, write the date, who called you, and who you called. Write the time of the call, what the call was about, and how long it lasted. Make notes such as, "Left a message" or "Talked about homework."

Don't let the phone log take the fun out of talking. It shouldn't be the main reason to call anyone. Let it happen naturally!

You can do it for a day, a week, or as long as you want. It will be fun to look back on it in the future to see who you were friendly with, what sorts of things were on your mind, and what you were talking about.

# #144. VOLUNTEER at the Fire Department

Although you might not be fighting fires with hydrants and hoses, your fire department may have other opportunities to let young people like you pitch in.

You don't have to battle fierce fires to make a difference in the fire department. Let the trained professionals handle the blazes, and you can handle the stuff they might be afraid of—like stuffing envelopes! If there's a firefighters' ball coming up, help out with the invitations. You could come up with design ideas or prepare the mailing (stuffing, addressing, stamping, and sealing envelopes).

Some other ways you can help out at the firehouse include offering to babysit the kids of firefighters on duty, getting a group of friends to help paint or clean the firehouse, or creating or improving the fire department's Web site.

The firefighters might even welcome volunteers to shine a fire engine or walk the Dalmatian! Woof!

You won't know how helpful you can be until you call. Be sure to use the main number, not an emergency number.

# #145. SHAKE UP Some SHAKERS

Shake up your family's dinner table—create one-of-a-kind salt and pepper shakers.

You can either spruce up the shakers you already own if your parents will allow it, or you can make new shakers. To make new shakers, save two small jars that you might otherwise recycle—for example, jelly or salsa jars. Be sure to save the lids.

Peel or soak off the labels, wash the jars thoroughly, and let them dry.

Decorate the outside of each jar by painting it and gluing on decorations like ribbons, googly eyes, or picture cutouts—let your imagination go. Just make sure that whoever uses the shakers has a way of figuring out which one is salt and which one is pepper. With a hammer and a nail (and an adult's help), poke holes in the lids. Fill each shaker with salt or pepper and screw on the lids. Let's eat!

# #146. Go on a WHALE Watch

The blue whale is the largest animal ever to live on Earth. It can be as long as a nine-story building is tall. Also, it can create the loudest sound of any living creature—even louder than a jet engine or a rock concert. Its call can be as loud as 188 decibels.

If you live or vacation near the beach, check to see if there are any whale-watching tours. The experience is unforgettable. Whales often come near the boats, and you can see them flap their fins and tails above water, come up for air, and maybe even leap (called breaching).

Because they are threatened by whaling, pollution, and the loss of their habitat, many whale populations are dwindling. Several species, including the blue

whale, are endangered. Whale-watching tours help people understand how beautiful and important whales are and that we should all work to help save them.

# #147. READ Palms

Want to know if you'll have a long life, if you'll be happy, smart, or rich? The answer is in the palm of your hand.

When you read the lines on a palm to tell the future, it is called palmistry, or palm reading. Dating back to ancient times, palm reading is still a popular method of divination (or telling the future). Palm readers usually charge you money to study your palm and explain what it reveals about your future, but with a little research, you can do it yourself for free.

See all those wrinkly lines on your palm? Although they differ from person to person, every hand shows four major lines: the life line, the heart line, the head line, and the fate line. Check out a book on palmistry to find out which line is which and what they tell you about your future. If your life line swings wide, for instance, it means you will travel a lot.

Remember, palm reading is not a science and it isn't always right. No matter what it might say on your palm, you are in charge of your own future.

# #148. ADOPT a Grandfriend

You're probably friends with a few older kids, but how much older are they? Make friends with someone who is sixty, seventy, even eighty years older than you are.

As people get older they get wiser, but they can get lonelier, too. If an older person has lost a husband or a wife, siblings, or close friends, they might need someone to talk to. Sometimes their families live too far away to visit regularly. A new friend might be just the thing they need.

So perk up someone's life and make a grandfriend. Check with a nearby retirement home and ask if there are any residents who would welcome a new visitor. Lots of older folks love talking to kids.

Ask your new friend about his or her life and family. What was it like when he or she was your age? Then tell him or her about your life, your friends, and your school. Try to visit regularly. You'll find that there are a lot of things you can learn from your new grandfriend, and you'll have fun!

# #149. CREATE a Menu

Chefs who create menus for restaurants have to sort in their minds through hundreds of types of foods and narrow the choices down to about a page's worth.

If you're tired of going to restaurant after restaurant and never finding what you like to eat on the menu, create your own menu with all of your favorite dishes.

Put together your favorite foods of all time on this ultimate menu. Include appetizers, soups, salads, main courses, desserts, and drinks. Go ahead and add anything you want, even if your parents never let you eat it or the dishes don't usually "go" together. If you want to have cheese in your cereal, do it. Fish-stick lasagna? Chocolate fajitas? No problem—it's your menu. Create an actual menu like the one they have in restaurants.

You might not get any restaurant to adopt your menu, but you might persuade your parents to let you cook your dream meal for dinner one night.

# #150. MAKE Trashy Art

Think you can only create art with some paint, a few paintbrushes, and a canvas? Think again! You can make anything into art—even trash.

Instead of recycling or throwing away your garbage, try transforming it into a work of art. Make a sculpture out of old bottles and cans, fashion a necklace out of gum wrappers, form a bracelet out of paper clips, cut up a magazine and create a mosaic—the possibilities are as varied as your imagination. Some other trash-turned-art supply ideas include cereal boxes, empty toilet-paper rolls, plastic bottle caps, scraps of fabric, newspapers, used envelopes—the list can go on and on.

With a little vision you can turn a random assortment of former garbage into a person, a car, a field of flowers, or something that exists only in your mind. Just think, you're making the world a more beautiful place with things most people don't think are beautiful.

# #151. ORGANIZE a Minithon

A marathon is a 26-mile race that takes hours to run, but a minithon is much shorter and can take minutes, even seconds to run.

Organize a minithon in your neighborhood. The distance can be however long you like—the length of your backyard, once around the block, or to school and back. Encourage everyone to wear proper running shoes and clothing, and have water on hand. Even if it's a short race, people still get thirsty. Make sure it's a safe route—not on a busy street—and it takes place during the day. To make it more interesting, don't have just running races. Have your participants hop on one foot, skip, or jump rope the course, too!

Give away prizes to all your participants, but make them small, just like the minithon—mini cookies, baby carrot sticks, or tiny toy cars.

# #152. LOOK for Symmetry

The word *symmetry* means equal sides. If you fold an object in half and find that each side is exactly the same, that object is symmetrical.

A square and a circle are both symmetrical. The human face is somewhat symmetrical, although there are minor variations—usually one eye is a little bigger than the other, or you may have a freckle on one side but not on the other. The opposite of symmetrical is asymmetrical.

Turn on your symmetry radar and walk around your house. See what symmetrical items you can find.

A computer screen? Maybe—but is there a company logo on one side only? A mirror? Yes (but the reflection, no). A book? No. A window? Most likely yes. Furniture like chairs and couches are often symmetrical.

To make a perfectly symmetrical piece of art, smear some paint on the center of a page and fold it in half. Unfold it to find a balanced image—it may be a blob, but it's a symmetrical blob.

Then go hang your picture on the asymmetrical fridge.

# #153. SING the Blues

If you're feeling sad or low, don't keep those feelings bottled up inside you, let 'em out and sing about it.

The blues are all about expressing how you feel, no matter how sad or down-trodden you are. This style of music evolved from African-American slave songs, and its songs are usually about the hardships of life. Listen to a blues CD at the library or at home. The singing can be slow and sorrowful, and you can feel the singer's sadness.

We all have times when we feel blue—that's when you need to sing the blues. If you know a song whose music and lyrics fit what you're feeling, sing it like you really mean it. Go ahead and write your own blues song, too, and accompany it with some wailing on a harmonica.

If any of your friends are blue about anything, get a blues group together. You just might cheer each other up!

# #154. PLAY in Another Country

Tag, hopscotch, hide-and-seek, Simon says—these children's games are not only immortal but international. Many countries have their own versions of these games, although they're usually called by a different name.

In Germany, kids don't play Simon says, they play ducks fly.

Here's how: Everyone stands in a circle. The caller stands in the middle. When he or she calls out "Ducks fly," everyone flaps their arms twice. The caller continues to call out things that fly (such as, "Bluebirds fly," "Airplanes fly," "Flies fly"), and everyone flaps their arms twice. However, if the caller shouts out anything that doesn't fly (like, "Pigs fly," "Ostriches fly," "Houses fly"), and someone flaps, that person is out. The winner is the last bird standing.

For more worldwide game ideas, ask kids who have lived in foreign countries, check out books at the library, or visit www.gamekids.com.

# #155. PLAY an INSTRUMENT

Are you fascinated by the flute or dazzled by the drums?

Decide what instrument you want to learn and if you want to learn it at school or take private lessons.

Join the band if your school has one. If not, start your own!

Can't get hold of an instrument? You can still make music with your own built-in instrument—your voice. Join the chorus at school or a choir in your community.

# #156. MAKE Your Own Music

You can make music right in your kitchen!

Line up eight glasses and fill the first with a little water, the second with a little more, and so on. You can create an approximation of the eight notes of a musical scale, tapping on each glass with a spoon to make a musical tone.

Play your homemade instrument for your family or friends. Maybe you'll be good enough to enter your school talent show! Just don't drop those glasses—that's a sound you don't want to make.

# #157. HAVE Some REFUND Fun

Since you have to take out the garbage anyway, why not get paid for it?

In some states, used cans and bottles can be returned to the store or a recycling center for a refund (usually five cents per can or bottle). If you live in one of those states, you can exchange the cans and bottles your family normally recycles for a nice chunk of change.

Set up a special box next to your family's other recycling bins for collecting the returnable. To find out if a bottle or can is returnable, look for 5¢ REFUND somewhere on it, usually at the top. Every week, take your stash to the grocery store or recycling center and cash in.

Not only are you helping your bank account, you're helping the environment, too.

# #158. CAST Your Family's Movie

The next phone call you get could be from a Hollywood producer who wants to make your family's story into the next motion-picture blockbuster. You've got to be prepared.

Which famous performers do you think could portray the members of your family and the other people in your everyday life? Is Will Smith a dead ringer for your dad? Maybe he's more like Johnny Depp. Does your mom get confused for Nicole Kidman or Renée Zellweger? You can cast actors who look like your family, or you can cast actors who talk, move, or laugh like them, whether they look the same or not. You can also cast nonactors like rock stars, athletes, or politicians. Just don't cast your real folks—that's too easy.

Look through magazines for pictures of the actors that you've cast and cut out the heads. Then tape them over your family's heads in a family photo. It could be the start of the movie poster for the film.

Of course, the biggest stars will line up to play you, but if you had to choose, who would get the role?

# #159. Stay HEALTHY

You can't cure a cold, but you may be able to keep from getting one in the first place.

An easy way to try to prevent this common illness involves a very important invention called … soap. A cold is a caused by a microorganism called a virus. Often people develop a cold simply because they touched their nose, mouth, or eyes without washing their hands first. Breathing the same air as a sick person is not wise, but you are actually more likely to get sick if you put your unwashed hands near your face! So wash those hands every time you come inside, and after you've touched a lot of things. It takes less than a minute, but can prevent days, or even weeks, of illness.

Breathing through your nose can also prevent some kinds of illness. The nose has built-in bodyguards—all those little hairs and mucus. Sitting with your mouth hanging wide open allows more germs to have access to your tender throat and lungs.

Eating healthy foods rich in vitamin C, like oranges and spinach, can help keep colds at bay, too.

# #160. LEARN Phobias

Some kids are afraid of the dark, but that doesn't mean that they *all* have nyctophobia.

A phobia is a very strong, persistent fear. It can make someone afraid of something as innocent as going to bed (clinophobia).

A lot of people are afraid of sharks, but they still go to the beach. But someone with galeophobia is so afraid of being attacked by a shark that they probably would be too afraid to even set foot on a beach.

Although some phobias are decipherable from their names, others are harder to figure out. Can you tell what someone with musicophobia is afraid of? You guessed it, music. If you have chrometophobia, you aren't afraid of chrome—you're afraid of money.

### Here are some more:

books: bibliophobia
spiders: arachnophobia
water: hydrophobia
strangers: xenophobia
monsters: teratophobia
school: scholionophobia

being alone: monophobia or autophobia
heights: acrophobia
enclosed spaces: claustrophobia
train travel: siderodromophobia
number 13: triskaidekaphobia

# #161. VISIT Memorials

As Americans, we rarely lose sight of the men and women who have fought for our freedom. Sites and memorials paying tribute to them are found all over the country.

Most towns have some kind of memorial to hometown soldiers who have given their lives in battles, or to people who are famous in that town's history. Call your town hall or local VFW (Veterans of Foreign Wars) to find out where the memorials are in your town.

Washington, D.C., hosts many distinguished war and presidential memorials that are magnificent to visit. The Washington Monument (dedicated 1885, opened to the public 1888), the Jefferson Memorial (dedicated 1943), the Lincoln Memorial (1922), the Vietnam Veterans Memorial (1982), and the Tomb of the Unknown Soldier (1932) are just a few. At the Vietnam Veterans Memorial, you can make an etching of any names that mean something to your family. Visit the library or the National Park Service at www.nps.gov for more information on each memorial.

# #162. ERECT a Graffiti Wall

You shouldn't write on your bedroom walls unless you're covered ... unless the wall is covered, that is.

Designate one whole wall of your room as a graffiti wall. Cover an entire side of the room with a huge sheet of paper (brown or white butcher paper works well, as does wrapping paper with the white side up). You may need several sheets of paper to cover the wall. Grab some pens, markers, and crayons and invite your friends over to write on your wall.

Tip: Make sure the paper is thick enough so that the ink from the markers doesn't seep through and stain your wall!

Keep the pens and markers by the wall and ask anyone who comes into your room, including your family, to mark some graffiti on the wall. They can contribute anything they like: a song, a drawing, a self-portrait, a quote, or a poem.

# #163. OBSERVE Cloud Art

Think of the sky as a museum and the clouds as the sculptures. Except that unlike in earthbound museums, sky sculptures can change shape and even disappear altogether. Yet they are also breathtaking, just as man-made sculptures can be.

There are three common cloud formations: cirrus, cumulus, and stratus. Cirrus clouds are feathery or wavy. Cumulus clouds are big and puffy, like heaps of whipped cream. Stratus clouds are gray and layered and cover the whole sky.

Spend an afternoon with friends, on the grass, staring up at the sky. Do this when (1) it's not raining and (2) cumulus clouds are out. They are the most likely candidates to form art.

To see if you and your friends really think alike, tell everybody to bring a notebook and a pencil. Point out a cloud and have everyone write down what he or she thinks it looks like. Then compare answers. Did everyone say "wheelbarrow"?

If you look hard enough, you might even find your own face in the sky.

# #164. RACE with Paper Airplanes

Put your paper-folding skills to the test. Challenge a group of your friends to paper-airplane races.

When it comes to making paper airplanes, technique is everything. Check out some paper-airplane books at the bookstore or library. Depending on the way you fold the paper, your airplane can fly fast and straight, glide slow and smooth, or it could even make loops in the air.

Choose a pretty windless day. Get some friends together in your yard or at the park and let the races begin. You can hold many different kinds of races: whose plane flies the fastest, whose lands the farthest away, and whose does the best loop de loop.

Have several trials, too, to see if it's a plane's design, a thrower's touch, or just plain luck that makes a winner.

# #165. THROW a Surprise Party

The hardest part about throwing a surprise party is keeping it a surprise.

Choose a friend or a family member whom you'd like to celebrate and throw him or her a surprise party. When you send out the invitations, be sure to let everyone know that … *ssshh! It's a surprise!* They shouldn't breathe a word to your guest of honor.

The most important thing to do is to come up with a believable way to get your guest of honor to the party without him or her finding out about the surprise. Perhaps someone can take the person out to dinner. While they're out, have all the guests arrive and then hide right before the guest of honor comes home.

The party doesn't have to be a birthday party. It can also be a going-away or welcome-back party, a congratulations party, or a just-for-the-heck-of-it party.

It's an even bigger surprise—and very funny—if a surprise birthday party is thrown nowhere near the person's birthday! If his or her birthday is in November, throw a party in April. Nobody will see that coming!

# #166. SAVE Some Trees

Does your family go through dozens of paper napkins, paper towels, and paper plates every week?

Break your family's paper habit and save a few trees.

Ask your family to use cloth napkins instead of paper ones. Don't have any? Then make some! Cut squares (15 inches by 15 inches) out of an old sheet, bath towel, T-shirt, or any other soft, clean material. If you wish, add embroidery decorations or initials.

Next time you spill something, don't reach for a paper towel—grab a cloth one instead. And in place of paper plates, use real ones.

By using less paper, you'll be saving trees (and the animals that live in them) as well as cutting down on garbage in landfills.

# #167. TOSS a Rainbow Salad

Rainbows are not tangible—you can't touch or hold them. They're made of sunlight reflected in water droplets. Make a rainbow that you can touch, and even eat.

The seven colors of the rainbow are red, orange, yellow, green, blue, indigo (blue-violet), and violet. Find a vegetable that represents each of these colors and toss them together in a rainbow salad.

Tomatoes would work nicely for red, while carrots would be perfect for orange. Try zucchini or yellow peppers for yellow and, of course, lettuce for green. Blue, indigo, and violet will be a little more difficult. Eggplant? Purple cabbage? Use your imagination.

Once you've got all your colors, chop up the ingredients, toss, and serve your colorful dish.

# #168. TAKE the STAIRS

Without elevators, there would be no skyscrapers. Do you think people who work or live in high-rise buildings could walk fifty flights of stairs two, three, or four times a day?

Next time you have the choice between taking an elevator or taking the stairs, use your leg power to get you to the top and choose the stairs. Not only is it great exercise, there's also no waiting!

If you don't live in a city or a town with any tall buildings, you might not use elevators all that much. But you probably do use escalators—those moving staircases they have at the mall and in department stores. Ditch those, too, and hit the steps instead.

You might find it's a very good opportunity to think. An elevator ride might last thirty seconds, but a staircase climb might take three minutes. That's a lot of extra thinking time—and you thought you were only exercising.

# #169. CREATE a New Legend

According to legend, Count Dracula was a vampire from Transylvania who drank people's blood.

Is the legend of Dracula true? What about the legend of Sleepy Hollow with its headless horseman? That's the thing about legends—nobody can be sure if they are true or make-believe. Often, legends have some basis in fact. For instance, there was a count in Transylvania named Vlad the Impaler who did some pretty awful things to people, but was he a vampire? Probably not.

Create a legend of your own, either about your town, school, or house. Have you ever found strange animal tracks in your yard? Write a legend about a mysterious creature that leaves those tracks. Is there a room or closet in your school that you never see open? Create a legend about what is behind the door and why it remains unseen.

Use your imagination and make your legend bizarre but somehow believable, so that your audience is never sure if you are telling the truth or not!

## #170. BE a Reporter

Don't take rumors and stories at face value. Get the facts and dig after the truth like a real reporter on the beat.

Focus on an interesting local or school news story and try to find the "five Ws": who, what, where, when, and why. These are the basic questions reporters answer in the first paragraph of a news story. The rest of the article fills in the details.

Snoop around. Ask questions of people who would be able to give you an accurate answer. Suppose you are trying to find out if the rumor about a foreign-exchange student coming to your school is true. Don't ask your best friend; ask someone who will know for sure—the principal, for instance. Find out who the student is, what country he or she is from, where he or she will stay, and when and why he or she is coming.

# #171. THANK a Police Officer

Being a cop can be a pretty thankless job. For all they do—catching criminals, keeping the streets safe, and helping in emergencies—police officers don't get thanked half as much as they should be.

A police officer has an extremely dangerous job; the police put themselves in scary situations so that citizens don't have to. Take time to let police officers know that you appreciate the good job they are doing. Next time you see a cop, say something nice and let him or her know that you recognize how hard a job it is and that you are glad they are there to keep your town safe.

They don't take on such a dangerous job for the thank-yous, but it's still nice for them to hear.

# #172. PAINT Your Face

Halloween is not the only time you can paint your face. Some people do it for parades or sporting events. You can paint your face any day of the year.

A costume shop or department store will sell water-based, nontoxic face paint that washes off easily. Look for the label ASTM D 4236, certifying nontoxic paint. Never use anything that is not intended for skin. Test a bit of the paint on the inside of your wrist a day earlier to make sure you're not allergic.

Make a design on paper before you put a brush to your skin. That will help you avoid mistakes—but if you do make one, you can just paint right over it!

Clean your face. Then drape a towel over your shoulders and tie back your hair, if it's long. Follow the directions on the paint package and use a new brush. Later, wash your face thoroughly to remove the paint.

Throw a face-painting party. Have a face painter at the party or ask everyone to show up with their faces already painted.

# #173. SURVEY Frogs

All over the planet, frogs and toads are disappearing and scientists aren't sure why. Help solve this environmental mystery by participating in a frog survey.

Because frogs and toads breathe and drink through their skin, they are especially sensitive to air and water pollution, as well as the sun's ultraviolet rays. If there is anything wrong with the environment, frogs are one of the first creatures to be affected.

Many frog and toad species like the Yosemite toad and the Great Basin Spadefoot frog are declining even in nature preserves and national parks. Other species like the Northern Leopard frog and the Pacific Tree frogs are also showing up deformed, with extra legs or missing eyes.

You can help scientists try to save our leaping friends by surveying the frogs in your neighborhood. Visit a nearby pond, stream, or marsh one evening a week for six to eight weeks and report back on what kinds of frogs you see, and whether or not they are deformed. To learn more about conducting a frog survey visit Frogwatch USA's Web site at www.nwf.org/frogwatchUSA.

# #174. SING Another National Anthem

Just about every country in the world has a national anthem, a song that expresses how proud and lucky its citizens are to live there. The only time you have probably heard the national anthem of another country is during the Olympic Games, when a gold medal winner's anthem is played.

Celebrate another country and take a shot at singing its national anthem. One place you can hear many different anthems is at: www.countryreports. org/anthems/nationalanthems.aspx

You can also get more in touch with our own national anthem. The words to "The Star-Spangled Banner" were written in 1814 by Francis Scott Key, but the song didn't become our anthem until 1931. Besides the well-known first verse that we all sing at school and sporting events, there are many more verses. Find a copy of the complete song at the library or online and try singing the whole thing!

# #175. PLANT Pennies

All it takes for some people to have a good day is to find a good-luck penny on the ground.

Take a handful of pennies from your piggy bank (look at it as an investment in happiness) and head for a mall or park. Plop yourself on a bench where lots of people walk by. When no one's looking, put a penny on the ground a few feet in front of you and then return to your bench.

Then watch to see if anyone picks up your penny. Most likely you'll see a smile on the face of the person who picks it up.

Once someone snatches the first penny, discreetly put a new one down and then sit back to get ready for your next good-luck victim.

You'll find that putting a smile on someone else's face is worth more than a hundred pennies.

# #176. CATCH a Snowflake

Snowflakes are some of nature's prettiest works of art. Each beautiful, delicate pattern is a one-of-a-kind masterpiece.

In the late 1800s a Vermont farmer named Wilson A. Bentley photographed thousands of snow-flakes and discovered that, like human fingerprints, no two are exactly alike. The next time it snows, try to test whether Mr. Bentley was right or wrong, by taking an up-close look at the falling white stuff.

The night before a predicted snowfall, put a piece of black construction paper into your freezer. This will be your flake catcher the next morning. As soon as the snow begins to fall, take your frozen paper outside. Stand in an open area and let the flakes fall on your paper. Take a look at the lacy designs covering your paper. Are any of them identical? Use a magnifying glass to see in even more detail, but don't breathe on the flakes—the hot air will melt them!

# #177. SAY HI to a Shy Person

There is a way around shyness, and that is you. You can make a shy person's day simply by walking over and striking up a conversation.

Even if you're shy yourself, work up the courage to reach out to someone you've never spoken to before. Everyone, even quiet and shy people, has something interesting to say. A lot of quiet people just need a little nudge, someone to make the first move, before they open up.

Another thing to think about: Most everyone is shy sometimes. Even a rock star, even the president, and even the loudest person in the world.

Not only will you inspire a shy person to go up to another shy person, you might even make a new friend.

# #178. KEEP a Diary

There are some things we don't want to talk about with anybody. That's what a diary is for.

Get yourself a blank pad and a pen and start to keep a written record of what you do and how you feel. You can get a special journal or a diary with a lock at a stationery store, or you can write in a notebook. What you fill your journal with is entirely up to you. Report about what happened at school today, write about what you want to do in the future, or express how you feel about a difficult situation or problem. Your journal is meant for your eyes only, so feel free to write whatever you want, even things you wouldn't tell anyone.

Don't throw away your old journals. It will be a blast to look back at them when you're older. You'll revisit all the people you had crushes on or disliked, and you might find you wrote about meeting someone for the first time who became your best friend.

# #179. ORGANIZE a Fashion Show

Let your friends strut their style on the catwalk. Organize a neighborhood or school fashion show!

You'll need a venue where the fashion plates can have an audience to walk by and impress. You can hold it in the school auditorium, a local theater, or even your own backyard or living room.

Decide on a theme for your show, such as Hot Fall Fashions, Casual Wear, or even something retro, like 1920s Cool. Ask your friends, neighbors, and classmates to be your fashion models and let them choose their own outfits, although they should go along with the theme. Now that you have the models, go and get your audience. Create flyers and send e-mails inviting people to come to your fashion show.

Before the big day, get your models together and hold a dress rehearsal, complete with music and lighting.

Fashions may go out of style, but fashion shows don't.

# #180. SINK Three Baskets

You may be one of those people who doesn't feel athletic, or who feels cursed with bad aim. Not so fast. Anyone—*anyone*—can make three baskets in a row.

By the way, that's not *weaving* baskets (although that, too, is possible). We mean throwing a wadded up piece of paper into a garbage can, or the equivalent. In the privacy of your own room, try it. Expect a few misses but commit yourself to victory. There should be no spectators so there's no pressure. If you feel any pressure, it's only what you're bringing upon yourself. Eliminate that. Relax yours shoulders and take a deep breath. Keep your eye on the basket. Throw!

Sinking every shot is not a guarantee even for you basketball players. Concentration is critical for everyone.

Maybe you'll do it on your first try. Don't be frustrated if it takes you a hundred tries, because when you do make it, you'll forget those ninety-seven misses right away. All you'll feel is victorious.

# #181. Run a Garage SALE

Whether you call them garage sales, tag sales, or yard sales, all you need is your old stuff that you no longer use.

Announce the date, time, and location of your sale by putting an ad in the local newspaper and on your town's Web site. You can also hang posters around the neighborhood.

Sticker all items with a price. People come to garage sales looking for bargains. Some will haggle for a lower price. Practice haggling right back!

# #182. HOLD a Swap Meet

If you don't believe that one person's trash is another person's treasure, sponsor a swap meet.

Announce a swap meet for a set day and time. Ask people to bring books, games, clothes, DVDs, or anything else they no longer want. Everyone checks out what everyone else brought and instead of buying, they trade.

You can also swap services, such as chores. For example, offer to rake someone's yard if they'll wash your bike.

# #183. DRAW from a Bird's-Eye View

Get a new perspective on things—try to see the world from a bird's point of view.

Drawing a house is easy. But try drawing a bird's-eye view of a house. It will look very different. A bird's-eye view is just what it sounds like—it's the way something looks when you're looking straight down at it, the way birds do when flying.

We don't often see bird's-eye views, even of everyday things. To see a bird's-eye view of a helicopter, for instance, you'd have to be directly above one (in another helicopter?).

**Draw each of these things from a bird's-eye view. Then add your own challenges to the list and ask your friends to try.**

| | |
|---|---|
| house | car |
| tree | bird |
| bike | dinner table |
| computer | yourself |

# #184. MAKE Riddle Cards

Next time you give someone a gift, have him or her expend a little brain power in order to receive it.

Create a series of riddles that the person must solve in order to find his or her surprise. Write the riddles out on index cards and plant them throughout the house. The solution to each riddle will lead the solver to the next riddle until the gift is found.

For the first card try something like "Go to a place where you can see yourself clearly." On a mirror, you will have taped the next riddle card! It might read: "You're always welcome here." Have the riddle card under the welcome mat, and so on. The last card leads your friend to the gift.

Make sure none of the riddles has the same solution, or the person might find the cards in the wrong order. Keep the cards as hidden as possible, so the person doesn't see one on the way to another.

You don't have to limit yourself to inside the house—you can get really daring and have cards in the yard!

# #185. WRITE Your Pet's Biography

The stories your dog or cat could tell you if he or she only knew how to talk—chasing squirrels, protecting your family from intruders, sleeping all day—what a life!

You may think your pets wait around all day for you to come home and play, but their lives are full of drama, intrigue, courage, and perhaps even romance. Since your dog or cat can't write, tell their stories for them—write their biography, or life story.

Be sure to include all the important milestones and life events—when your pet was born, whether he or she had siblings, who his or her parents are, the day he or she met you, and so on.

When you're done, you can have your pet sign, or paw print, every copy.

# #186. ORGANIZE a Combination Bee

Some people are really good at spelling, while others are good at geography. But how many people are good at both?

Organize a combination spelling/geography bee at your school and find out. Each participant (or team) must answer a geography question correctly, and then spell the answer for a bonus point.

Award participants or teams one point for answering the geography question right, and another point for spelling it correctly. The players with the most points at the end of the contest are the winners.

You can also combine subjects other than spelling and geography. How would you combine math and history? Or science and spelling? Experiment with all kinds of combination bees—you'll find out how well-rounded your education really is!

# #187. MAKE Snow Impressions

Most people know how to make a snow angel—lie on your back and slide your legs and arms up and down—but what other things can you imprint in the snow?

Try lying on your back and moving just one of your arms. Does it look like a tomahawk? A flag? Can you make a butterfly in the snow?

Don't stop at the supine (lying-on-your-back) position. Plop your body into the snow in different ways, even facedown! Or team up with a friend or a sibling. See what comes when you lie next to someone and move various limbs.

Go to an untouched field or your yard after a fresh snow and fill it up with your experimental snow impressions.

# #188. START a Goodwill Wave

When someone does something nice for you, don't keep that good feeling to yourself. Pass it on and do something nice for someone else. You might just start a wave of goodwill.

You don't need to wait for someone to be kind to you in order to start your goodwill wave. Get the wave going by helping someone carry their groceries, holding the door for the person behind you, picking up something someone has dropped, giving someone flowers or a nice note, or any other act of kindness.

Let the person know that you are starting a goodwill wave and ask them to pass it on and do something nice for someone else. Hopefully your kind gesture will start a domino effect that will last a long time.

# #189. VISIT the Closest Town You've Never Seen

Any place you haven't been to yet is a mystery waiting to be solved or a surprise waiting to be discovered—even if it's just a small town on the other side of the woods whose name you see on street signs.

Plan a pilgrimage to the town closest to your own that you've never visited. Maybe there's a nice park to picnic in, or an historic library to browse through. On the surface, the neighboring town may not seem so different from yours, but each town has its own story. Even if their library is not very historic, make that one of your first stops and see what is of interest locally.

Every so often, take another trip to the new closest town you've never seen. Over time, you will increase your boundaries considerably, and you'll see a lot of places that you never knew were so cool. Or so different ... despite first impressions.

# #190. BE Prepared

"Be prepared" is the Boy Scouts' motto, but it's a good idea for anyone—boy or girl, child or adult.

We all have moments when we wish we had a pen to write a phone number down, an adhesive bandage for a cut, or a photo of our pet to show a friend.

Every time you have such a wish, don't get frustrated. Just prepare yourself so it won't happen again. Put that pen, a couple of bandages, or the photo in your knapsack so that you'll always have them.

Other useful items are: any medication you need to take regularly, tissues, a map of your town, a list of important phone numbers, and even a good book in case you find yourself with a little time to kill while waiting somewhere.

### More ways to be prepared:

- ◎ Get a spare set of eyeglasses made.
- ◎ Leave an extra house key with a trusted neighbor approved by your parents.
- ◎ Have candles and a flashlight with batteries on hand at home in case of a blackout.

# #191. LOOK UP State Names

Pennsylvania was named after its founder, William Penn. What about the other forty-nine states?

Several states are named for European kings or queens (Louisiana is named for French King Louis XVI, and Maryland is named for Britain's Queen Henrietta Maria, who was called Queen Mary). Some are named for places in Europe (New York and New Jersey). Lots of state names come from Native American words, like Massachusetts, North and South Dakota, and Michigan.

Find out the origin of each state name in the country. Books, Web sites, and state tourism offices will have the information.

Try matching a few to get you motivated. Answers are at the bottom.

| | |
|---|---|
| Michigan | A. Spanish for "snow-covered mountain chain" |
| Connecticut | B. Aleut for "mainland" |
| California | C. Chippewa for "a great water" |
| Nevada | D. name of a fictional island in a Spanish novel |
| Alaska | E. Mahican for "beside the long river" |

*Answers: Connecticut, E.; California, D.; Nevada, A.; Alaska, B.; Michigan, C.*

# #192. CALL a Radio Station

You don't have to have a hit single to hear yourself on the radio. Lots of radio stations listen to their listeners and put *their* voices on the air.

Your best bet to get your voice on the air is to call when the station is holding a contest or asking for audience opinions. But that's often when the lines are most busy. Some stations ask listeners to call in with song requests or dedications—you can try then, too.

Use your phone's redial button and try to get through. If it's busy, keep hitting redial. Depending on the time of day and the station, it may take a while. Especially if they're giving away money or concert tickets!

You might even want to think of something witty to say if there's an opportunity. After all, fame doesn't come knocking every day.

# #193. INVENT Synonyms

Swift. Rapid. Speedy. Quick. "Zoopst."

All those words are synonyms for fast, even the last one, although it's made up. But it sounds fast, doesn't it?

A synonym is a word that means the same as another. Make a short list of some of your favorite nouns and adjectives. Then make up a word or two that sounds like it could be a synonym for each word on your list. Have a dictionary handy to double-check that the word you create doesn't already exist.

Now write a short story using your new words. Make sure you use each new word in context so your readers don't go "Huh?" Instead of having a character say, "That's a cute woofle," have him say, "Your woofle barks much less than the woofle next door." That way your reader has some idea what a woofle is—it's probably a dog (or some other pet that barks!).

Let a friend read your story and see if he or she can figure out what each of your synonyms mean.

# #194. REACH OUT Across Your Neighborhood

On May 25, 1986, six million people formed Hands Across America, a human chain from New York to California, holding hands to raise awareness about homelessness.

Organize a similar stunt in your own neighborhood or town to raise money for a local cause. When people sign up, ask each of your hand-holders to make a one-dollar donation. Give each person a number that they can pin to their shirt on the day of the event. That will be their place in line.

Your hand-holding chain can stretch across the entire town, or even just across a park or around a school. If the route involves roads or private property, you might need a permit from the town. Call the town or city hall and briefly explain your idea. Your town may even want to get involved as a sponsor.

Specify what time everyone should be in place on the day of the event, and then have event coordinators along the line blow whistles at the particular time when everyone should join hands.

# #195. DRAW the Unseen

Just because you've never seen something doesn't mean you can't draw it. That's what your imagination is for.

Parts of the oceans, the jungles, and the universe have never been seen by the human eye. What could be living there?

Find these mysterious beings or places in your mind and transfer them to paper. Draw something you've never seen, and may never see. What kind of creature could survive at the bottom of the ocean where no human has ever been? Would it have good eyesight to see through the blackness, or a hard shell to protect it from the pressure of the depths?

And what type of life-form could exist on a planet in another solar system? First of all, what kind of other planets are out there?

When you draw the unseen, it becomes the seen—and you become the first person ever to see it.

# #196. WALK Down a Cloudy Beach

Sure, nothing beats going to the beach on a hot summer day. But the beach is a great place to go in all kinds of weather.

Don't limit your beach-going to warm summer days. Whether it's rainy, cloudy, cold, or even snowing, the beach is one of the most relaxing places to be.

Enjoy the mood of a beach on a cloudy or rainy day. Take a long walk and, if it's not too cold, take off your shoes. You will see that it doesn't matter that it's not sunny. The waves are still calming, the sand is still soothing, and the view is very peaceful.

One thing's for sure, it won't be crowded.

# #197. SPEAK Backward

Gymnastics mental some try. That's "Try some mental gymnastics" with the words reversed. There's also "Yrt emos latnem scitsanmyg," which is the same sentence, but with the *letters* reversed!

Speaking and reading backward—whether you're switching around words or letters—is like doing gymnastics with your brain. Ask a friend to practice speaking words backward with you. Keep in mind there will probably never be a time when you'll need this skill, but it's fun to see how quickly you can switch everything around in your mind.

Write notes backward. Answer backward. Read these familiar phrases and try to repeat them backward, but without looking at them:

- ◙ What is your name?
- ◙ The dog ate my homework.
- ◙ Would you like fries with that?
- ◙ I pledge allegiance to the flag of the United States of America.

Try saying other familiar phrases backward without first looking at them—it's even harder that way.

# #198. LIST Your Island Top Five

If you were stranded on a desert island without any hope of seeing another human for years (or ever!), what would you want to have with you?

Make a series of lists of the top five things that you couldn't live without: five foods, five books, five DVDs, five photos, five articles of clothing, and more. Keep an "Island Top Five" notebook, and every few months take another shot at remaking your top five lists. You'll notice that your loyalties may have changed since you made your first list.

After you've made your top five lists, try to narrow your choices down to three, and finally to just one. One kind of food for the rest of your life? Better make it good!

# #199. LEARN CPR and the Heimlich Maneuver

Cardiopulmonary resuscitation (CPR) is a procedure aimed at restoring normal breathing and heartbeat to anyone who has stopped breathing or has had a heart attack. Giving CPR involves applying pressure to the chest to massage the heart and performing artificial respiration (mouth-to-mouth). This includes tilting the victim's head back, pinching the nose, making a tight seal over his or her mouth with yours, and blowing in air in short breaths.

The Heimlich maneuver helps someone who is choking. It involves reaching around the victim from behind, making a fist and clasping it with the other hand just below the victim's rib cage, and suddenly thrusting upward to dislodge whatever is stuck in the windpipe.

Call your local chapter of the American Red Cross and ask when you can take a class or get a lesson in both procedures. It's vitally important that you learn from and practice with a professional. What you learn could someday save someone's life.

# #200. BUILD a Stone Wall

The very first construction project was probably a stone wall. The builders didn't need cranes, cement, or a zoning permit, and neither do you. But you do need adult permission. And a good site.

With friends or family, plan a rugged day of old-fashioned stone-wall building. Stone walls are handsome, useful (for dividing lawns from woods, for example), and, with teamwork, easy to build. Look for nice places in a friend's backyard or your own. Find a location near rocks, so you don't have to do any long-distance hauling. Use sticks as markers to plot roughly where you want the wall to be.

You will need gloves and a wheelbarrow to carry the rocks to your site.

Use any rocks that you like, as long as they are not too round, and pile them into the wall any way you want.

Your wall can be tall or short. Remember, even one that's just a few stones tall can look very nice. In other words, don't feel you must outdo the Great Wall of China.

# #201. MARBLE on Paper

We all know that oil and water don't mix, but they can get together to create some gorgeous works of art.

Did you ever notice how salad dressings made with oil and water always separate no matter how many times you shake the bottle? Or that after a rainstorm, puddles in the road often show a glossy layer of oil on top? Oil and water are unable to mix and will always separate themselves into layers.

You can use this property to create marbleized paper, using a shallow baking dish, water, and some oil-based paints. Before you begin, be sure to cover your work area with old newspaper.

Fill the baking dish almost to the top with water. Pour some oil-based paint into the water and watch the two liquids separate. Stir to create a swirling pattern in the paint. Place a sheet of paper onto the surface of the water and lift it off right away. Paint side up, place the paper on newspaper to dry. Your paper will have a bright, swirly design that looks like marble.

# #202. PLANT Mistakes

Throw a few errors into the next story you write, give the story to a friend, and ask him or her to find the mistakes.

There are many types of mistakes you can include. Spelling mistakes are easy to sneak in. Mispell words that are not so obvious—for example, *misspell* was spelled wrong in the first half of this sentence (without its second *s*!).

Throw in some grammar and punctuation mistakes, too. "Forget" to capitalize a person or place name. Don't use a comma when you should. Use the wrong verb tense—for example, write "She saying yes" instead of "She said yes."

---

**The trickiest mistake you can plant is a factual one. Write "He had fifteen cents in his pocket—only a dime and quarter" instead of "He had fifteen cents in his pocket—only a dime and nickel." Give your friend a nickel for every mistake he or she catches, but ask for a dime for every one he or she misses!**

---

# #203. MAKE Name Cookies

Try this recipe for peanut-butter cookies, but rather than using cookie-cutter shapes (such as circles, stars, or bunnies), roll the dough into small logs. Use them to form the letters that spell out the names of your family members.

## PEANUT-BUTTER COOKIES

4 cups flour
¼ teaspoon salt
1 tablespoon baking powder
1 cup creamy peanut butter

1 cup (2 sticks) softened butter
1 cup dark brown sugar
2 eggs
⅔ cup corn syrup

Sift flour, salt, and baking powder together and set aside. In a separate bowl, beat peanut butter, butter, brown sugar, eggs, and corn syrup until smooth. Slowly add flour mixture and blend to form a smooth dough. Wrap and refrigerate for at least 2 hours.

Preheat oven to 325°F. Roll out dough into ¼-inch-thick logs. On an ungreased cookie sheet, form letters out of the logs. Bake for 8 to 10 minutes.

# #204. MAKE and Take a Rorschach Test

To learn more about yourself, stare at a blotch on a page. Sounds strange, but this is a psychological exercise called a Rorschach test.

Hermann Rorschach was a Swiss psychiatrist who devised the test in 1921. In a Rorschach test, a person looks at a series of ten standard inkblot designs and says what he or she feels about each. Based on a person's responses, psychologists make interpretations about his or her personality and intelligence.

You and your friends can make Rorschach tests and interpret what you see. Make them by smearing paint in the middle of a piece of paper, folding it in half, and quickly unfolding it so that you get a symmetrical blob. Use any colors you want, and as much or as little paint as you want. If someone looks at an inkblot and sees an airplane, you could interpret that to mean that person likes to fly. Or if someone sees a turtle, that might mean the person is shy and likes to stay in his or her shell.

There are no right or wrong answers, and no good or bad blobs.

# #205. WATCH Things Decompose

Do you want to know what life is like in a landfill? Even if this doesn't sound like the most engaging topic, it's good to know how long it takes trash to decompose in the soil.

A landfill is a huge hole in the ground where the garbage you throw out every day gets dumped. Once about ten feet of trash has been laid down, the hole gets covered by a thin layer of clean soil, followed by more waste.

To see just how fast (or not so fast!) things break down in the soil, try this experiment. Take a piece of a vegetable, a piece of paper, and a piece of a plastic cup and bury them in your yard or in a box of dirt on your windowsill. Water the area and leave it. Come back after a week and dig each item up.

What happened to the vegetable? To the paper? To the plastic? Try waiting another week and see how everything changes again. This should give you a hint about what's happening in landfills across the country.

# #206. CREATE the Secret Behind a Secret Identity

Superheroes and spies all have secret identities—everyday personalities that hide the fact that they have superpowers or dangerous secrets.

What if you were one of those secret identities—if your everyday life was covering up a wild and dangerous hidden life like that of a spy or a superhero? What kind of life would that be, and why would you need to cover it up?

Create the hidden life that your secret identity is hiding. Perhaps you are a scientist studying an average American family (yours!), or maybe you were wrongly accused of a crime and you are hiding out as a regular schoolkid. You might be a spy from another country or an alien from outer space pretending to be a kid.

What is your name in your hidden life? How would you change between your everyday life (your secret identity) and your hidden life. What happens if someone sees you or figures out who you really are?

# #207. FLIRT with Fireflies

When male and female fireflies flicker their lights, it's their way of saying, "Hey, baby, let's get together!"

A female firefly stays still and flashes her light at a passing male. The male replies with a flash, and the two communicate like this until the male lands near the female.

On a warm summer night, watch for a firefly light. When you see one, wait two seconds, hold your flashlight near the ground, and flash it for one second. If the firefly comes over to investigate, it is male.

# #208. CATCH Fireflies

Fireflies are also called lightning bugs. They may be bright like lightning, but they're not fast as lightning.

Punch small holes in the lid of an empty glass jar. Head for the twinkling over the grass. Fireflies move slow enough that it shouldn't be hard to scoop one into your jar and put the lid on.

Observe the bug up close for a little while, but then let the little flasher out so it can put on another show.

# #209. KNOW Your Blood Type

A and B aren't just grades—they're blood types. So are AB and O.

Your body can accept only certain kinds of blood, based on what your blood type is. It's important for doctors to know your blood type in case you need to donate blood or to receive a transfusion.

Type O blood is called the universal donor, because anyone can receive type O blood. If you have type O, though, that is the only blood type you can receive. People with type A can accept O and A blood, while people with type B can accept O and B blood. Type AB is called the universal recipient, because someone with this type can receive any other blood type.

Do you know which blood type you have? Next time you visit the doctor, find out. You can also test it yourself (with an adult helper). Self-tests are available at drugstores. Be warned, though, testing for your blood type involves pricking your finger, so if you get squeamish at the sight of blood, you might want to stick with asking your doctor.

You don't have to travel to the exotic Caribbean and suit up in scuba gear to find sunken treasure.

Invite friends over for an excursion beneath the surface of a backyard pool. Toss a handful of coins into the water and watch your treasure plunge to the bottom. It's not lost forever. Make teams or play one-on-one to see who can retrieve the most money.

Throw a few wild cards into the pool as well—things that you can pretend are more valuable pieces of treasure. As long as it's waterproof and heavy enough to sink, it's fine. Don't use anything potentially dangerous, like pens that can leak or glass bottles that might break.

Speaking of danger, there are no sharks or pirates, but you still must use precaution during the hunt. Make sure you have adult supervision and make sure everyone puts safety first. That means, jump in one at a time and always pay attention to everyone else when you do jump in (so you don't collide!).

# #211. DRAW from Memory

Without looking at a banana, try drawing one. Easy, right? How about drawing a book? No problem. Okay, now try drawing a dentist's chair. Not so easy.

Things that we see every day, like bananas and pencils, are pretty simple to draw without looking at a model. And although most people have seen a dentist's chair (and hopefully sat in one for a checkup!), we see one only about twice a year (unless we're dentists). It's difficult to remember enough details to draw a dentist's chair without looking at one first.

For the next few days, look a little longer at things you might not be able to draw from memory, like a snowmobile, the T-shirt your best friend wore to school yesterday, the mailbox at the house on the corner. Then try to draw them from memory. If you study something and try to remember how it looks, you'll have better luck trying to draw it.

# #212. ASK "What if?"

Have you ever wondered how different your life might have been if things hadn't happened the way they did?

Ask a bunch of what-if questions about yourself and your life. You'll have lots of fun coming up with answers and imagining a world that might have been.

What if you had been born in another country, or even on another planet? How would your life be different? You'd speak another language, for starters, and you'd eat different foods. What kind of clothes would you wear? Would you go to school for more years or fewer? What kind of house would you live in?

What if you could be given the ability to fly but you had to give up the ability to walk, or to speak? Would you do it? What if you could be one of the first people to colonize Mars, but it meant you could never come back to Earth? Would you go?

Get a circle of friends together and ask each other what-if questions like these. You might be surprised at your friends' answers!

# #213. PICK Apples

Whether you go for a Gala or relish a Rome Beauty, apple picking is an ideal way to spend an autumn afternoon.

Apple orchards are found throughout the United States. Most apples aren't ready for picking until fall, although you can find some action in the spring and summer, depending on where you live.

If there are no apple orchards in your area, try picking another kind of fruit or vegetable. There are pick-your-own peach orchards, pear orchards, strawberry patches, pumpkin patches, cornfields, and more.

Choose a beautiful fall day and with a basket or sack and a bushel of friends head for the nearest orchard and pick the day away. The orchard air will be clean and crisp—just like the apples!

# #214. PRODUCE Your Life's Soundtrack

Did you ever notice the music playing in the background during a movie or television show? That's the soundtrack.

A movie or show's soundtrack can affect how you feel as you watch. Sad music will make you feel melancholy during good-bye scenes; triumphant music will lift your spirits as a character wins a race; music that gets louder and more frantic will make you feel nervous as a character is chased by the bad guys. The moviemakers choose certain music to tug at your heartstrings or make your heart race.

Record a soundtrack for your own life. What songs express how you feel right now? What song would you play as you walk to school? Play sports? Eat dinner? Choose any kind of music you'd like—classical, blues, hip-hop, rock and roll, opera, whatever suits the situation.

Make an MP3 playlist with your soundtrack and give it a name.

As your life changes, your soundtrack will, too. So make a sequel track every year.

# #215. VOLUNTEER for a Campaign

If you ask people in public office how they got started in politics, chances are pretty good that they'll say, "By working on an election campaign."

Even though you might not be old enough to vote, you can still make a difference at the polls. Check out where the candidates in your area stand on local issues. If you believe in what one of them says, find out how to help on his or her campaign. There are lots of things you can do to help get your candidate elected, such as creating campaign buttons, stuffing envelopes, distributing flyers, or handing out T-shirts.

Once you become active on a campaign, you'll have lots to talk about with your parents and other adults. Discuss the issues that are important to you, and tell them who you'd vote for if you could. You can even hold a mock election in your school. Make up ballots and have your classmates vote for their favorite candidates.

Each time you breathe out, you release a puff of carbon dioxide into the air. Unless your breath is really awful, this doesn't affect those around you.

Ants, however, are an exception. No matter how many mints you've eaten, the smell of your breath will terrify them! An ant's antennae detect the carbon dioxide in your breath and perceive it as a threat. See for yourself how frightened a community of ants can get just because you're breathing.

Breathe gently on an ant (no need to empty your lungs out on the poor thing!). It will get scared and soon communicate its panic to the rest of its colony. Alarmed, the other ants will come to its defense and search for the intruder. If no other breathing attacks are delivered after several minutes, the ants will think that all is safe again and go back to their usual ant activities.

# #217. MAKE a Life-Size Maze

One of the most famous mazes is the labyrinth in Greek mythology, in which the Minotaur, a creature with the body of a man and the head of a bull, devoured anyone who dared to enter.

You don't need a Minotaur to have a good maze. In fact, if you have a basement or a recreation room piled high with stuff, you could make a very good, Minotaur-free maze.

It takes a crafty mind and some manual labor to assemble a working maze, and you'll need a lot of items to make even a short maze. Did anyone you know recently move? Ask for the leftover boxes to form part of the maze. You can also use couch cushions, bookshelves, chairs, small tables, blankets, old posters, and almost anything else that's big enough. Since most of the items that you'll use as walls won't be very high, you'll have to crawl, rather than walk, through the maze.

# #218. JOIN a Club

The Society for the Preservation and Encouragement of Barber Shop Quartet Singing in America is a club. Puzzle Buffs International is another. And, of course, there is Ducks Unlimited.

These three examples alone should prove that there is a club, organization, association, society, or group for everyone and every type of interest. You may find that you can belong to more than one of them.

Spend a little time in the library and online looking for clubs and groups of people who love what you love. Most have toll-free phone numbers, and many have Web sites. Some may offer free membership, and others might require a fee.

Just be sure that if you want to join both the Professional Rodeo Cowboys Association and the National Association of Watch and Clock Collectors, that they don't meet at the same time.

# #219. LEARN to Juggle

Pictures on the walls of Egyptian tombs and drawings on early Roman and Greek pottery show that jugglers have been livening things up at parties since ancient times.

To learn how to juggle, you'll first need to practice catching. Gently toss a ball, an apple, or a beanbag, if you have one, back and forth between your hands. Focus on tossing carefully. Good throws make for good catches! When you think you're ready, try using two balls. Toss the ball into the air from the right hand to the left hand. When the ball is at the highest point of its arc, toss the other ball to the right hand. Practice this until you've mastered it.

Now you're ready for the fun part—juggling with three balls. Hold two in your right hand and one in your left. Toss the same way you did with two balls— whenever one ball is at the highest point of its arc, toss the next one. With lots of practice, you'll be able to juggle with all kind of objects!

# #220. DRAW a Tattoo

The nice thing about art is that if you lose interest in it, you can just take it off the wall. It's not so easy to take tattoos off your arm, although it can be done with lasers. Consider a painless and less permanent alternative: draw a tattoo.

For ideas, look at people's arms, ankles, or shoulders—some of the most common tattoo sites. People often get tattoos because they feel the image says something about themselves. People with tiger tattoos might think of themselves as strong and fearless, while those with flowers might see themselves as sweet and beautiful.

Decide what you'd like on your tattoo. Snakes and dragons are favorites, as are hearts, flowers, or fish. Your tattoo can be whatever you like, as long as it says something about you.

On paper, draw and color your tattoo design. If you like, cut it out and tape it to your skin like a real tattoo. Unlike a real tattoo, though, you can just take it off if you get tired of it (or if your parents freak out).

# #221. FOLLOW a Trail

Animals don't intend to have humans follow the trails that they leave. Most of the time, they'd rather just be left alone.

If you have the urge to test your detective skills, try following the trails of another type of animal—a couple of your friends. You can track your friends in a park, a familiar area of woods, or even along sidewalks.

Pair up and give two people a fifteen-minute head start. As they go, the first pair should leave subtle clues to show their way, such as footprints in the dirt, a row of pebbles across the path, a stick stuck in the ground, or a small pile of rocks.

After the fifteen minutes are up, you and your partner start tracking. Keep your eyes and ears open (the pair ahead may have trouble keeping their voices down) for clues to where they've gone.

Take turns being the tracked ones and the trackers so that everyone has a chance to sharpen his or her powers of observation.

# #222. PLANT a School Garden

Do you love recess? Do you love the great outdoors? Then you'll definitely love this project!

Make your school yard a place you'll really want to hang out in during your spare time. Pick an area on your school property that could use some special attention. Any overlooked patch of ground will do.

Talk to your teacher and organize a class-wide cleanup. Here are just a few things you can do: plant flowers, rake up leaves, pick weeds, repaint a bench if there is one, put up a bird feeder, and paint a four square court on the ground. You can even ask for donations from local businesses to help spruce up the area. Stop by the hardware store and see if they'll donate a trash can and a recycling bin.

You'll make this corner of the Earth one that's nice for everyone to enjoy.

# #223. MAKE Juice Pops

Do you like your juice cold? Really cold? How about frozen?

On a hot summer day nothing is more refreshing than a frozen ice pop. You don't need to buy them, though. You can make them yourself in your freezer. You can buy ice-pop molds at a housewares or discount store, or you can make your juice pops with an ice-cube tray, some plastic wrap, and some toothpicks. You're in control of the flavors. Any kind of fruit juice works—orange, apple, cranberry, grape, and so on.

Fill the ice-cube tray with your chosen juice. Cover the tray tightly with plastic wrap. Poke a toothpick through the plastic wrap into the center of each cube so that it is standing straight up. Carefully place the tray in the freezer and wait for your pops to freeze. It will take a couple of hours. Then take your frozen treats out of the freezer and cool off!

# #224. RE-CREATE the Pony Express

From April 1860 to October 1861, the daring Pony Express riders delivered mail along the 1,800-mile stretch between Saint Joseph, Missouri, and Sacramento, California.

The system could get the mail from end to end in ten days, each rider handing it off to other riders at posts along the route.

Re-create a kind of Pony Express in your neighborhood. See how quickly you and a bunch of riders can get a letter from one end of town to the other. Ask a group of friends to be volunteer Pony Express riders. They'll help you deliver your letter across town on their bikes.

Station your riders at intervals along the mail route. Write a letter to a friend who lives across town. Mark the envelope "Pony Express," and note the time. Ride your bike to the first station and pass the letter to the next rider. He or she will deliver it to the next rider, and so on, until your letter reaches its destination. You'll probably do it in less then ten days, but then you don't have as far to go!

# #225. BE a HERO

Even if you don't jump through flames, you can still be a hero every day just by making others feel good.

It doesn't have to take a disaster or an emergency to bring out the hero in you. All it should take is a careful eye and a little sensitivity.

Give your seat on a bus or train to an older person, or even to a younger person who looks tired. Donate some of your allowance to a worthy cause. Help an older person carry groceries. Tell someone that his or her bag is open. Any one of those actions might be the nicest gesture someone gets all day, and for that, you're a hero.

Other heroic acts are more anonymous. You'll be a hero to movie-theater employees if you throw your empty candy box in the trash, not on the floor. Or if you see that someone left the lights on in his or her car in a parking lot, ask a store employee to make an announcement. You will save someone a lot of aggravation.

# #226. RUN a Taste Test for ANTS

Diet sodas contain artificial sweeteners like aspartame that are meant to taste like sugar. While humans might be fooled, ants definitely aren't. Have a taste test, and see for yourself just how sharp these little guys are.

Get two cans of the same type of soda, one flavored with sugar and one flavored with aspartame. Go outside and find an anthill. Since ants are everywhere, finding an anthill shouldn't be too hard. Put a couple of drops of each drink on a hard surface close to the anthill, leaving more than six inches between samples. Remember which is which! Watch and wait. Soon the ants will come for their sweet snack. Which drink will they go for?

Unless the ants are watching their weight, they'll skip the diet soda and head straight for the one that contains real sugar—their nourishment! Ants don't know everything, though. They are fooled by drinks sweetened with saccharin.

# #227. SOLVE a Mystery in Your Life

There are lots of mysteries still to be solved in the world—Bigfoot, Amelia Earhart's disappearance, Roswell aliens....

Solving mysteries takes hard work and sometimes training. Some people devote their entire lives to solving one spooky thing or another.

However, you don't have to go that far. You don't need to rent a submarine, carry a machete, or brave Arctic winds to get the facts on whatever mysterious occurrence interests you. Choose a mystery in your own life. It may be finding out what your great-great-great-great-grandfather did for a living, who ate the last brownie, or what happened to all of your missing socks.

Make a list of all the possible solutions to your mystery. Don't rule out any theories unless you're completely sure they aren't possible. Conduct interviews with family or friends who might have been around when the mystery took place or who might have clues. Listen well, and keep notes on any clues you find.

A good detective is a careful detective.

# #228. CHOOSE to Walk

Next time you need to get somewhere that's not too far away, skip the ride and walk there instead.

Have you and your family gotten into the habit of hopping into the car to go just about anywhere, even a few blocks down the street or around the corner? If so, kick your automobile dependency and go for a ride on the ankle express! Let your built-in foot and leg power get you to your destination.

If your parents need to get just a few items from the store, volunteer to make the journey—on foot. Or if you live close enough, set your alarm early and walk to school instead of taking the bus. With each step, you'll be saving energy and resources, and getting exercise at the same time.

# #229. INVENT a Board Game

There's no shortage of great board games, but that shouldn't stop you if you have an idea for a new one.

Create your game board and cards on a piece of card stock or other material that's stiffer and more durable than paper. You can cut off one face of a cereal box and use the inside of it. You'll need pawns for the players, so rummage around for the right ones. Old thimbles, action figures, coins, toy cars, or paper clips would work. Use dice or a timer if the game requires them. Write out the rules and directions and explain them to friends. Put the pawns in the Start box and give it a try!

If you are stuck for an idea, go through the games you like and figure out why you like them. Take elements from different games and combine them.

Learn about how to copyright your game at the library or on the U.S. copyright office Web site at www.lcweb.loc.gov/copyright. If you think you've got a real hit on your hands, propose your idea to toy companies.

## #230. GROW Plant Cuttings

The next time you need to give someone a present, give a gift that's really alive—a cutting from a houseplant!

Lots of houseplants are just like starfish. If you cut off a branch (or an arm, in the case of the starfish), a whole new plant can grow from the cutting. Before you go snipping up all the plants in the house, however, make sure you first check with whoever owns the plants!

With a pair of scissors, snip off a small branch from the plant and stick it in a jar of water. In a few days, roots will begin to sprout from the cutting. Before you give your new plant as a gift, make the jar more festive by decorating it with paints or other trimmings. Let your gift recipient know that once the roots appear, the plant can be repotted.

# #231. DESIGN a Book Cover

Your favorite book and your favorite book cover aren't necessarily the same. (That must prove that you really shouldn't judge a book by its cover.)

Take a book down from your shelf and redesign the cover. You can choose a book whose cover you don't like or one whose cover you do like.

Before you begin, read the book again. Do any events, characters, or feelings stick with you after you've finished? Would any of these make a good cover image? The main point of a book cover is to get people's attention so that they pick up the book and want to read it. (It just shouldn't give away the ending!)

Sketch out your idea for the cover design. How large will you make the title and the author's name? Create your design on a piece of paper the same size as the book's actual jacket. When you're done, fold your cover over the book. Now the only thing left to do is to put it back on the shelf!

# #232. DRY Your Own Fruit

Fruit is one of the healthiest things you can eat. We're supposed to eat two to four servings a day.

The trouble with fruit is that you've got to eat it right away or else it spoils. Unless, of course, your fruit is dried! If you haven't got time to eat all your fruit before it goes bad, try drying your fruit first and eating it later.

Making this treat requires no energy (except your own) and creates no waste. Peel an apple, core it, and slice it into ½-inch rings. Then thread them onto a piece of clean string and hang them up to dry. After a day, the apple rings will get dry and rubbery. Keep them in a tightly sealed container until you're ready for a snack.

Try drying pears and pineapples, too!

## Some things to keep in mind:

◎ Make sure that you do this in a very dry place—it won't work well in humid conditions.

◎ Be sure the fruit is really dry before putting it into a container—otherwise you may find that your snack starts to grow mold!

◎ It's a good idea to check your fruit a few days after you've sealed the container to make sure it's still mold-free.

# #233. COMMIT to a Book

Book some time with a book. With school, chores, family, and friends, it can be hard to find enough time to read for pleasure. Pick out a book you've been eager to finish and commit to reading at least one chapter every night. Depending on the length, you could finish the book in record time, and be looking forward to the next one.

Breaking down a big book into manageable chunks will make it seem less challenging and more enjoyable to read!

# #234. START a Book Club

You probably never thought of reading as a team sport, right? Find a group of friends who like reading and talking about books and make a book club!

As a group, decide on a book that you want to read. If you all can't agree, each person should take a turn choosing the next book. You can share copies or borrow them from the library.

When everyone is done reading the book, meet to discuss it and ask questions. Book clubs are about expressing your opinions, so it's OK to disagree!

# #235. LISTEN to Steel Drum Music

To some people, the melodious sound of the steel drum reminds them of a Caribbean breeze or a tropical sunset.

The steel drum was invented on the Caribbean island of Trinidad in the 1930s. This instrument is made from the head of an empty 55-gallon oil drum that's been hammered and shaped to produce musical tones. Although it began in the Tropics, the steel drum is now popular throughout the world. Steel drums, also called pans, are a huge part of West Indian music called calypso.

It takes more than ten years to master the art of making steel drums. They look deceptively simple, but the drums are finely tuned instruments that can carry the full range of musical notes. Check your local library for CDs of steel drum music, or poke around online for samplings. You may feel like you've instantly been transported to a land of palm trees and parrots . . .

# #236. GO to SUMMER CAMP

Camps are not just for tents and bugs anymore. And you no longer have to choose only between day camps or overnight camps.

You can go to a traditional sleepaway camp with tents, campfires, and sing-alongs, but you can also choose a camp that focuses on your favorite activities. There are computer camps, basketball camps, art camps, bike camps, and even space camps. Of all the different kinds of camps, there is probably one that concentrates on one of your interests. Or a camp may inspire you to take up something new.

If your parents usually choose where you go to camp each summer, lend a hand this year. Poll your friends about camps they've gone to or heard about. If there is a part of the country or world that you'd like to see, find out if there are any camps there. Books about camps are available at the library or bookstore. You can search online, too, at the American Camping Association's Web site at www.acacamps.org.

You might have as much fun choosing a camp as attending one!

# #237. HELP with a Move

Just for fun, pack everything you own into boxes and lug them across town. Oh, that doesn't sound like fun? Well, you're right—for most people it's not.

Next time a friend or relative has to pack and move, offer to help. When everyone works together, packing can even be fun. Besides, hard days of packing and moving often end with a relaxed, spontaneous pizza party!

One way to speed up the packing process is by making a short assembly line. Have one person stand at the bookshelf and remove books, handing them to another person who packs them into the box. That way the packer doesn't have to stand up and bend over for every book. The same goes for kitchen stuff and clothes.

When you stoop down to lift things, be sure to bend at the knees and not at the waist so you don't strain your back. Never attempt to lift something too heavy; wheel heavy boxes on a dolly instead. If you're tired, stop. Tell as many jokes and stories as possible to make the day more fun.

# #238. LEAD a Back-and-Forth SING-ALONG

When you like a new song, you probably start to remember the lyrics after only a few listens. So it should be easy to remember every *other* word of the lyrics, right?

With a friend, choose a song you both know by heart. Then sing it—but without the song playing in the background. And without singing in sync.

Instead, alternate words. For example, if your song is "Twinkle, Twinkle Little Star," one person will sing "twinkle," the other will sing the next "twinkle," the first will sing "little," the second will sing "star," and so on. See how fast you can go before someone trips over his or her tongue.

For a greater challenge, choose a faster song. Or play the game with more than two people, but the alternating rule still applies—so if there are three of you, each will sing every third word, and so on.

You may find that when it comes to singing lyrics, less is more ... tricky.

# #239. WRITE Reviews

Nobody has time for bad entertainment. That's why there are reviewers. And you will find that it is just as much fun to write reviews as it is to read them.

Pick a book, movie, music album, video game, Web site, television show, or anything else you'd like to share your opinion on. Let people know how good (or how terrible!) you think it is. Remember, you can choose anything from restaurants to in-line skates.

A review is a lot more than a summary of what happened in a movie or a book or what kind of food you ate at a restaurant. Reviews are all about opinions, so don't be shy about yours. The most important part of a review is "why." If you loved an album or a video game, let your readers know why it's so great. If you didn't like something, use your review to tell others why they should avoid it. Don't just say you loved or hated something. Give reasons for the way you feel.

# #240. HELP a Missing Child

Thanks to photos on milk cartons and computer screens, many missing children are not faceless anymore.

In 1984 the National Safety Council began distributing photos and statistics (name, age, date, location of disappearance, etc.) of missing children. They did this on milk cartons so everyone who had cereal for breakfast (meaning a lot of us) would see these faces and names.

Now anyone with a computer can see what missing children look like, which will help them be on the lookout for a tip-off that could help law enforcement. The National Center for Missing and Exploited Children offers a free, downloadable screensaver at www.missingkidsaver.com, which provides the same information displayed on milk cartons, but more of it.

Anytime you see such a photo, look at it for thirty seconds. Learn the face and name as best you can. You just may be the next person to see this missing child.

If every kid reading this book does this, maybe more missing children will be found.

# #241. TEST the Pollution Level

Did you know that two-thirds of the people living in cities around the world breathe unhealthy air?

With so many cars, trucks, and factories in our country, even if you don't live in a city, your air is still not free of pollution. To find out how clean (or not clean) the air is in your neighborhood, try this simple experiment.

Smear three sheets of plain white paper with petroleum jelly. Place two of the sheets outside, either taped to a windowsill or tacked to a tree in your yard. Keep the third sheet inside. After a day, bring one of the sheets of paper inside. See how much dirt collected in the petroleum jelly? That's air pollution, and you breathe it in every day. Bring the other sheet in after a week. It's probably even grimier. How do your outside papers compare with the paper you kept inside?

Now that you've seen air pollution firsthand, you may want to write to your local government or to the editor of your local newspaper, expressing your concern about air quality in your neighborhood.

# #242 DRAW a Reflection

A reflection is like a shadow, because it's always tagging along, especially when you're near a smooth, clear surface. Light is needed to produce a reflection. That's why you see yourself in mirrors during the day a lot more than at night!

Find a photo of something being reflected in a mirror, window, puddle, or anything else. Do you notice how it's reversed? That's the tricky part about drawing a reflection. You're not just drawing something twice; you're drawing something as it is normally positioned and as it appears flipped in the reflection, with the right and the left sides reversed.

Try drawing your face and its reflection. Here's a handy tip to orient yourself: If your nose is pointing left in actuality, it will be pointing right in its reflection. The tips will face each other.

If the tips face in the same direction, you've got a broken mirror!

# #243 CLEAN Naturally

While you're cleaning the house, why not help keep the Earth clean at the same time? Make natural cleaning products, and eliminate the hard-to-recycle plastic packaging from store-bought products.

The ingredients for an effective cleaner are probably right there in your kitchen cupboards. For a simple cleaner, add ¼ cup of sudsy ammonia, ¼ cup of vinegar, and 1 tablespoon of baking soda to 1 gallon of hot water. Then you can really clean up! Surprise your parents by cleaning the kitchen. Or really shock them by cleaning the whole house!

You can also avoid a trip to the store by using old T-shirts and towels as rags instead of buying new sponges and paper towels.

By using homemade cleaners, you will not only be helping save the planet, but you'll also be saving money.

# #244. RE-CREATE Famous Images

Neil Armstrong setting foot on the moon. Six marines raising a flag on the Japanese island of Iwo Jima during World War II. The four Beatles walking across the street on the *Abbey Road* record-album cover.

These are just a few of the familiar images that most people have seen before and can recognize. Some of these are images of real events (the moon landing and the Iwo Jima flag raising), while others are artistic creations (the album cover).

With a camera, a group of friends, and a list of ideas, re-create these and other famous images from history and art. Any book on famous images of the twentieth century (of photographs and film stills) or a general book on art history would give you lots of ideas. Once you and your friends are posed, snap the photo.

We may not have any actual photographs of some famous events in the past, like George Washington crossing the Delaware in 1776, but you may be able to find paintings of these events. And if not, you can imagine what they might have looked like and then act them out.

# #245. FIND Your Town's Oldest House

Houses can last a long time. There's probably proof of that right down the block, or even next door.

Track down the oldest house in town. Some historic houses have placards either on the front lawn or near the front door stating when the house was built. If you've passed houses with these signs, write down the addresses and dates. One of them may have been the former home of someone famous. Nevertheless, other houses in town may be just as old or older. How do you find out which is the oldest?

Call your local historical or preservation society or your town's chamber of commerce—they may already know which house is the oldest. You can also check your public library or contact your town or city hall.

# #246. RACE Elevators

You don't need a driver's license, a helmet, or even a road to participate in this race. Actually, just about the only thing you do need is luck.

Next time you and a friend are in a building with more than one elevator, race them. Each of you must get in on the same floor and head for the same destination. As in any race, the first one there is the winner. You will encounter two types of races, solo and variable.

Solo is when you're lucky enough that no one else gets into the elevator during the race. If you both race solo, you'll find out whether or not the elevators move at exactly the same speed.

Variable is any race in which other people use the elevator while you're racing it. Don't be frustrated when your elevator stops on other floors to pick up or drop off people. That's the variable, and it's part of the race.

Just make sure you never get in the way of people who are not racing.

Or maybe they *are* racing....

You'd better do *something* about that smell. Even if you don't think your clothes smell, sachets are great to keep in your dresser.

A sachet is a small pouch filled with sweet-smelling herbs and flowers that help eliminate stinky odors in your drawers, bathroom, backpack, closets, kitchen, or anywhere else! They're the most natural air fresheners around.

To make a sachet, cut off the foot of an old pair of nylon pantyhose. Make sure it's clean and it doesn't have any holes! Stuff the foot with a bunch of herbs, dried flowers, or spices. Try different combinations, and see which you like best. How about roses and rosemary, or lilacs and cinnamon? Tie the open end of the hose with a ribbon.

If you hang your sachet in the bathroom, steam from a hot shower will release the scent. You can put sachets in your dresser drawers or, better yet, inside smelly sneakers. They also make terrific gifts!

# #248. GO on a BACKYARD Bug Safari

The Earth is crawling with insects. If you added up all the bugs in the world, their weight would be twelve times heavier than the weight of all the humans!

Go on a backyard bug safari to find out just how many creepy crawlies call your lawn home. Mark off a small square (about 12 inches by 12 inches) of grass in your yard, using four sticks and some string. Now get down on the ground and begin your bug hunt.

At the grass-and-dirt level, look for crawling insects like ladybugs, beetles, and ants. You may even see some resting fliers like bees, flies, or mosquitoes. Take a twig and dig a little deeper into the soil to find pill bugs and millipedes. (Millipedes and centipedes are arthropods—insect cousins, not actual insects.)

In your one square of dirt you'll find carnivores and herbivores, predators and prey, and probably some strange critters that you've never seen before.

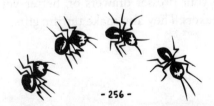

# #249. MAKE Your Own Potato Chips

Don't skip the chips the next time you have a snack attack!

Store-bought potato chips are high in fat because they're fried. All that extra fat is bad for your body, and the potato-chip packaging is bad for the Earth. Every time you and your friends scarf down a bag of chips, you're not only filling your stomachs, you're also helping fill a landfill with the throwaway bag. Instead of creating more trash by eating packaged potato chips, make your own eco-friendly, lower-fat munchies!

With your parents' help, slice several potatoes into very thin slices. Brush them with vegetable oil, and broil them in the oven until they're crisp. For variety, try using red potatoes or sweet potatoes instead of regular spuds. You can also make chips using other vegetables, like carrots, and even fruit, like apples. Combine several different kinds of chips for a tasty, colorful snack! Because these chips are broiled, not fried, they are less fattening than store-bought varieties.

# #250. RUN a Taste Test

Once, two major soda companies pitted their colas against each other in a national taste test to see which brand people liked more.

Pick any two brands of the same kind of food or drink and conduct a taste test of your own. You can compare corn muffins, orange juice, tuna fish, mustard, ketchup, pickles, pizza, yogurt, cheeseburgers, ice cream—anything you want. Try to stick with just two brands of each food—any more than that and people have a hard time keeping tastes straight. Once you've decided what you'd like to test, go to the grocery store and stock up on your samples.

Blindfold your testers and ask them to taste one brand and then the other. Ask which they prefer and record your results. At the end, count the votes and reveal which brands won. Are you surprised?

# #251. INVENT a Secret Handshake

Most of us don't spend much time thinking about handshakes. There are essentially two kinds—a firm one and a flimsy one.

But strength aside, handshakes involve ten fingers, so there are a lot of possibilities. Don't settle for the regular grip—make your own shake for you and your friends.

Experiment with possible ways to shake. You could shake with only your thumbs, or with your finger extended to touch the other person's pulse. You could just clasp fingers instead of smacking palms. Or lock pinkies.

The handshake you decide on has to be comfortable and easy to do quickly. And be selective about whom you share it with. Otherwise your secret handshake won't be a secret for long!

# #252. ORGANIZE a Carpool

Acid rain is a form of air pollution that causes smog in industrialized areas, erodes structures, damages crops and forests, and depletes freshwater lakes of life.

The problem of acid rain started in Europe back in the late 1700s, during the Industrial Revolution. Since then the problem has only worsened. Acid rain forms when sulfur and nitrogen from factories and car emissions combine with air moisture to form acids that fall to the ground as rain. Every year millions of tons of sulfur dioxide and nitrogen oxides are emitted into the atmosphere in the United States. Every car on the street contributes to the pollution and so adds to the problem.

How can you help? Start by organizing a carpool! Find kids in your neighborhood who get separate rides to the same school each day. Set up a rotating schedule so that different drivers take turns. You can even organize carpools to sports practice and the movies. The fun comes from knowing that you're doing something to help save the Earth! Ask your parents to consider carpooling to work, too.

# #253. READ from Every Section of the Newspaper

Reading a newspaper (whether online or on actual paper) is an important everyday routine for many people. People rely on their daily paper as a source of accurate information—on everything from what's happening in distant countries to the weekend's weather forecast.

The next time you're eating breakfast, instead of looking at the cereal box, grab a copy of that day's newspaper. Try to read at least one article from every section. You'll be amazed at how much interesting information you'll pick up.

If you're up for an extra challenge, try this with the Sunday newspaper. It's usually meatier than the daily paper, and packed with lots of extras, like book reviews, a magazine section, or even coupons.

Newspapers aren't only about serious stuff—lots of them have comic sections. Make sure you read the funnies. Otherwise you might be missing out on some serious laughs!

# #254. HOST a FAMILY Quiz Show

People love testing their own knowledge against quiz-show contestants—and, of course, imagining they are winning the money!

Host a quiz show that gives you and other members of your family an edge on winning—make it a family-trivia quiz show. Take some time and come up with forty or so different quiz questions about your family. For example: What year was your sister born? Where did your family go on vacation two summers ago? What was your first word? What did your grandma give your dad for Christmas last year? What size shoe does your older brother wear?

You can also group the questions by category (Vacations, Birthdays, Mom, etc.) and difficulty level.

Now gather up the contestants—your family, of course—and have them test their knowledge about the people living with them. Don't let your face give away the correct answer—try to keep it blank when reading the questions. The winning prize can be that the loser in each round has to do the winner's chores the next day!

# #255. Go WORM Watching

Worms spend most of the daylight hours in underground burrows. At nighttime, they surface for a snack of dirt and grass.

Make a worm fiddle, and bring these slimy wigglers out during the day. A worm fiddle is made of two sticks, each 1½ feet long. To make yours, ask a grown-up to whittle a point at the end of one stick, and then to carve notches every couple of inches along the other stick. Plant the pointy end of the first stick into a moist spot on the ground. To make worm tunes, you'll need to play your worm fiddle like a violin or cello. Draw the notched stick across the smooth stick in the soil. This will create rhythmic vibrations underneath the ground.

Keep this up for several minutes. The vibrations in the soil will make the worms think there's some sort of danger underground. Pretty soon, they'll come to the surface looking for safety. If your fiddling doesn't attract any worms, try another spot in the ground.

Around 3100 BCE, Egyptians began documenting history using a picture alphabet called hieroglyphs.

For hundreds of years no one knew what the hieroglyphic pictures and symbols on Egyptian tombs and temples meant. But a big rock called the Rosetta stone provided a key to help decode the writing. Found in 1799, the stone is carved with the same inscription in three different alphabets: hieroglyphs, an Egyptian alphabet called demotic, and Greek. Using the known Greek, scholars were able to translate the mysterious hieroglyphs.

Hieroglyphs can sometimes stand for an entire word; for example, a hieroglyph of a dog can mean "dog." Or hieroglyphs can stand for syllables or sounds, and a group of hieroglyphs can spell a word. Hieroglyphs can be written up or down, and usually from right to left. There are no vowels or punctuation.

To instantly translate your name (or any other word) into hieroglyphs, visit Egypt's tourism Web site at www.touregypt.net/ename/.

# #257. SEE Yourself Grow

Keep your personal photo documentary in an album to show others how you changed from a sweet, innocent child to a sweet, innocent older child.

On the first day of the month for one year, take a photograph of yourself first thing in the morning when you're looking in the mirror (or have someone else snap it for you).

Whether you get dressed, brush your teeth, or brush your hair first is entirely up to you! On a piece of paper, write the date with a felt-tip pen and hold the paper up as the photo is snapped. That way you'll know which picture is from which day.

After the year is over, look at your twelve photos. You'll be able to see how you gradually changed as time went on. Your hair may have gotten longer and longer (or suddenly shorter, if you had it cut). You may have lost a little more baby fat (if you still had any to begin with!). You may even have begun to look wiser! Or perhaps you will not have changed at all.

# #258. TURN Your School into the World

With your teacher's help, plan an International Day at your school during which every class must become a different country. Have a sign-up sheet with a long list of possible countries so that there are no duplicates.

On International Day itself, every classroom should be redone as the country it is representing. If it's a country nestled in the mountains, draw mountain ranges on the chalkboard or hang up pictures of mountains. Serve food and drinks from that particular country, dress in traditional garb, learn a folk dance, and learn a few phrases, like "Hello," "Good-bye," "Please," "Thank you," and "My name is."

Before International Day, every student should make a passport so that he or she can travel from country to country (or classroom to classroom). Model your passports on actual ones, and use real photos of yourselves. Students can travel the world by going from one classroom to the next with their passports. Take security seriously—travelers without passports should not be admitted to any foreign country!

# #259. SAVE a Wolf

Due to relentless hunting from the 1930s to the 1960s, wolves almost disappeared in America. In 1973, the U.S. Endangered Species Act made killing certain threatened animals (including wolves) a crime.

Save more wolves by writing to your Congressional representatives to tell them that wolves need consistent protection. Start a petition in your school demanding support of wolf-reintroduction programs.

For more information, check out the North American Wolf Association at www.nawa.org.

# #260. SAVE a Tiger

Tigers are in danger because people hunt them (even where it is illegal) and cut down the forests where they live.

Tigers need your help! Write a letter to the leaders of India, China, Russia, or other nations where tigers live, urging them to enforce laws protecting tigers from being killed.

To learn more about what you can do to help, check out Save the Tiger Fund at www.savethetigerfund.org.

# #261. DRAW a Shadow Portrait

Find a model and a dark room, and make a shadow portrait!

Ask your model (a friend or family member) to sit about a foot away from a blank wall in a dark room. Since this will be a profile portrait, the model should be facing sideways. Tape a piece of black paper to the wall near your model's head. Set up a flashlight or a desk lamp so that it shines directly at the model's head and creates a shadow on your black paper. With a white pencil, carefully trace the outline of your model's shadow. Make sure you've chosen someone who can sit perfectly still for at least a few minutes. You'll never be able to trace a fidgety shadow.

When you are finished tracing, carefully cut out the portrait and glue it onto a piece of white paper. Now your model will be able to see his or her shadow anytime!

# #262. MAKE a Music Video

To make a great music video, you'll need a video camera, creativity, and the latest chart-topping music act. If they're not available, your friends should do just fine.

You can make your own video version of a song by your favorite band, or you can make a video for a song you wrote yourself.

Get together with your "band" and figure out what will happen in your video. Will it have a plot that the band will act out, or will your video be concert footage showing the band playing for a crowd? For costumes, go down to your local thrift shop or Salvation Army store and buy used (and inexpensive!) clothes. Be sure you hold a few rehearsals before you start rolling the cameras.

If you made a video for a song that you didn't write, consider making a copy of the video and sending it to the real band. They might not use your idea for their next video, but they'll certainly be flattered that you interpreted their song.

Have you ever wondered what it's like to be a fish? Going snorkeling is one way to find out what life is like beneath the waves. Put on your bathing suit and jump in!

All you need to explore under the surface is a snorkel and a pair of goggles. Fins are useful, too, because they help you swim faster and farther. A snorkel is a J-shaped tube with a mouthpiece. While you are swimming, the tube sticks out above the surface, and you can breathe through the mouthpiece. If you don't have this equipment, see if you can borrow it from someone. Otherwise, it's pretty inexpensive to rent.

Once you've checked out the underwater scene from the surface, put on your goggles, fit your snorkel to your mouth, and jump in. Don't let the top of your snorkel go underwater, though, or you'll get a mouthful of $H_2O$.

# #264. RECITE a Famous Speech

When he was inaugurated as President of the United States in 1961, John F. Kennedy told the American people, "Ask not what your country can do for you, ask what you can do for your country." These words still inspire us to keep striving to better our country. Visit the library to find other well-known speeches. You can listen to celebrated speeches at: www.history.com/video.do?name=speeches. Choose one that means something to you and learn it by heart.

Only the speeches made in the last hundred years or so have been recorded. So we'll never know exactly how Lincoln sounded when he gave the Gettysburg Address, but we can imagine.

### Here are a few speeches you might want to check out:

**Abraham Lincoln's Gettysburg Address**

**Winston Churchill's "Iron Curtain" Speech**

**Martin Luther King, Jr.'s "I Have a Dream" Speech**

**Barack Obama's inaugural address**

# #265. PLAY the "The" Game

*Any* word game can be the "The" game.

Twenty Questions is an example. Think of something, say, a palm tree. Your partner asks questions.

1. "Is it a person?"
   "No."
2. "Is it a thing?"
   "Yes."
3. "Is it something in the room?"

Oops! Out, and with seventeen questions left to go! Why? Because he used the word *the*.

No matter what the game, anyone is automatically out if he uses the word *the* as part of the game play.

A game called crambo is another good example. This is a game where one player says a line and the next player must rhyme it.

Player 1: "Every day I go to school."
Player 2: "And hope that I don't break a rule."
Player 3: "When I come home I jump in the pool."

Player 3 is out—but he wouldn't have been if he had jumped in "a," "that," or "our" pool.

# #266. CONTACT an Old Friend

Don't let old acquaintances be forgotten—get in touch with some friends you haven't heard from in a long time.

Maybe you've moved to a different town and it's been a while since you've seen or spoken with friends in your old town. Maybe you made friends at camp, but they live far away. Or perhaps there's a kid in school you used to play with when you were younger, but for whatever reason you've drifted apart.

Surprise one of them with an out-of-the-blue phone call, letter, or e-mail. It's always fun to find out what someone has been up to and see how life goes on even when you're not there.

You don't have to get in touch only with old friends; you can also surprise your faraway family members. If your grandparents, aunts, uncles, or cousins live too far away to talk to every day, call or write when they'll least expect it.

It's never too late to get back in touch with someone—it's as easy as dialing a phone!

# #267. BOB for Apples

Bobbing for apples isn't an exclusive Halloween activity, although that's when it typically happens. You can bob for apples anytime, wearing a costume or not.

Fill a clean, wide tub with drinkable water. You can use a large soup pot, a bathtub, or a kiddie pool. Remove the stems of some fresh apples, rinse thoroughly, and toss them in. Make sure the apples are not too hard. Softer apples are easier to grab with your teeth.

All bobbers should clasp their hands behind their backs and try to grab an apple with just their teeth. Take turns, so you don't end up bonking heads! Once your mouth touches an apple, that's the one you must keep going for until you sink your teeth into it.

If you want a water-free alternative, leave the stems on and tie the apples to strings. Then hang them from a bar or a tree branch and go for the apples in the same way.

# #268. ATTEND a Powwow

A powwow is a social occasion for Native Americans to get together and wear traditional clothes, dance, sing, eat, and laugh.

Experience the rich traditions of the first Americans—get yourself to a powwow and check it out. Powwows are held all the time throughout the country. To find one near you, contact a local reservation, a Native American center, or an intertribal association. Also, a local college may have a Native American students' association that holds powwows or can tell you where to find one.

At the powwow, try the food, listen to the music, look at the crafts, and watch traditional dances like grass dances and fancy dances. Powwows are sacred events, so it is very important that you always ask permission before taking pictures, bring your own seats (the benches are for the dancers), and stand during songs when others stand.

# #269. TEST Truth in Advertising

How many raisins do they say are in the box of raisin bran? How many chips are supposed to be in each chocolate chip cookie?

Most people don't check these things. Rather than take advertising claims at face value, investigate just how accurate some of those promises are.

Pay close attention to advertising claims for a few days. Write down any that you read in magazines or see on TV. Then test a few.

Many cereal companies make raisin bran. Find one that says it provides a certain number of raisins per scoop, or bowl, or box. Check to see if the claim matches reality. Pour the full box of cereal into a big dish, then pluck out all the raisins, counting as you go. It's good to have a counting partner, in case you lose track.

You can do the same with chocolate chip cookies, chunky tomato sauce, non-crumbling potato chips, or any other food about which promises are made. Be sure to get permission before handling the food and disrupting the kitchen in your crusade for the truth.

# #270. FIND a Pen Pal in Another Country

What's it like to wake up to a herd of thundering elephants or have winter in July? Write to a kid in another part of the world and find out.

To find an international pen pal, ask your school or house of worship if they have a pen-pal exchange program. Or you can read up on the place that interests you and write to a school or youth organization there, asking for a pen pal.

Whether you choose an e-mail pen pal or a snail-mail pen pal is entirely up to you. E-mail has made finding and talking to people around the globe easier, faster, and cheaper than ever. When online, just be sure to never give out your home phone number or address to someone you don't know. While e-mail is quick, there is nothing like getting a letter in your mailbox.

If you take the time to find and correspond with a pen pal, you could end up with a lifelong friend (not to mention someone to visit if you ever travel to Melbourne, Moscow, or Mozambique).

# #271. MAGNIFY Yourself

Get to know your body's own landscape—with a magnifying glass. Your body is just as interesting as lush forests and rugged prairies. When you get really close, you'll notice that the Earth's landscape and that of your body look remarkably similar.

Grab a magnifying glass and take a look at the skin on your arm. What are those holes? They are your pores. Sneak a peek at your skin when you get goose bumps. Your skin will look like a mountain range or the surface of another planet.

Stick out your tongue and look at it in a mirror through the magnifying glass. You'll experience a close encounter with another alien landscape, only wetter! Ask a good friend if he or she wants to get to know the real you, up close and personal, and maybe he or she will return the favor. It's hard to check out your own hair! But you will find peach-fuzz meadows on your face, streaks of lightning in your eye's iris, cool grooves on your fingernails, and much more. You're a wild world.

# #272. RUN a Delivery Service

Make some extra cash. Be a gofer!

If you are friendly with your neighbors and live in an area where shops are within walking or biking distance, you and a couple of friends can set up an after-school or weekend gofer (go for this, go for that) service. Distribute flyers or e-mails to your neighbors announcing your new service, what kinds of things you can deliver, your hours of operation, and the phone number where customers can reach you.

Some things people will most likely want delivered include prepared foods, things from the supermarket, dry cleaning, newspapers and magazines, and office supplies. Sure, your customers can call the stores directly to get these things, but since you and your friends are so nice, you'll have a personal connection, as well as the ability to run several errands at once.

> You can charge a fee per item or a flat fee per trip. Or you may not want to charge anything, since you'll probably be tipped every time.

# #273. ORGANIZE a Triathlon

A triathlon is a three-part race in which athletes swim, bike, and then run. The Olympic triathlon includes a .9-mile swim, followed by a 24.8-mile bike ride, and finally a 6.2-mile run. The most grueling triathlon is the Ironman, in which athletes swim 2.4 miles, bicycle 112 miles, and run 26.2 miles. It is an incredible test of physical endurance.

Get together some buddies and organize a triathlon of your own. You don't have to try for the Ironman (and you really shouldn't, unless you are very well trained) or even for the Olympic distances. You might try four laps in a pool, a 2-mile bicycle route, and a ½-mile run. Or you could make it very short: swim once across the pool, go around the block on your bike, and run once around your house.

If swimming, biking, and running aren't your thing, do three other physical challenges in your triathlon. Maybe you have to bounce down the block on a pogo stick, make ten baskets at the basketball court, and then cartwheel from one basket to the other.

# #274. VISIT a Broadcasting Station

Take a trip to a local television or radio station and find out exactly what goes on behind the cameras and microphones.

Call the station and ask if it gives tours or allows visitors. Most television stations broadcast only the news at the local studio. Other shows are filmed ahead of time and fed into the station via satellite. Ask if you can watch during the daily newscast. If you are visiting a radio station, you may be able to meet your favorite disc jockeys and even watch as they broadcast their show.

If you live near or visit Los Angeles or New York, you have a lot more options. Lots of game shows, talk shows, and sitcoms are filmed in those cities, and they all need live studio audiences. One way they make sure they get a full, lively bunch every day is to give the tickets away for free. Tour guides and Web sites provide numbers to call for the free tickets.

On some shows, they might even request volunteers from the audience—and you could appear on TV!

You can make your own simple animated "film." All you need is a small pad of paper and a pencil.

To create a sheep walking for example, draw it on the right side of the last page of the pad. On the next page, draw the same sheep a little to the left, with its two front legs above the ground, as if it were lifting them to start walking. On the third, draw the sheep a little farther to the left, this time with all of its legs off the ground. Continue until the sheep has crossed the entire road—uh, page. Then, using your thumb, flip the edges of the pad. It's animated! The more images you draw and the closer together you draw the movements, the smoother the animation will look. Flip backward to see the sheep cross the road in reverse.

Experiment with more complicated actions—like two people playing catch, or someone fishing, or a rocket ship taking off. Whatever you draw has to be near the bottom edge of the pad or else you won't be able to see it when you flip the pages.

# #276. Put INVENTIONS in Chronological Order

Which came first, the toaster or the CD player? If you don't know off the top of your head, it's easy to look it up.

Take a pencil and a pad of self-stick notes and scour the house for modern—or not-so-modern—marvels. Label each item with the year or decade that you think it was invented. What year do you think the microwave was invented? What about the electric stove? Do you think the dishwasher was invented before or after the sewing machine?

Once you're done, go back and number the items in order, based on the years you wrote on the labels, from the earliest to be invented to the most recent.

Now check each item's history in a dictionary, an encyclopedia, or on the Internet. Are you surprised at how long something has been around, or how recently it made its appearance? It's hard to imagine kitchens without microwaves, but how new are they? You may be surprised to find that some things came about earlier than you guessed.

# #277. FOSTER Frogs

You can watch frogs hatch from eggs, grow into tadpoles, and finally into adult frogs!

In some places, it is illegal to collect frog eggs. If this is not the case where you live, walk to a pond in the spring or summer.

Look for a mass of jellylike eggs near the plants at the edge of the water. Only if there is a big bunch of eggs, scoop a few into a clean jar along with plenty of pond water. Put your eggs and pond water in a large bowl or fish tank. *Never* add water from the tap. Add some rocks that come up above the surface (the tadpoles will crawl up there when they grow their legs). Change the water with fresh pond water every few days.

In a week or so, the eggs will hatch into tadpoles. They'll grow back legs first and then front legs a few weeks later. You'll need to cover your bowl or tank with a screen so your new hoppers don't escape! A few weeks more and their tails will start to shorten. When they do, return the frogs to the pond.

# #278. Skip STONES

You can't make stones run, but you can make them skip.

At a large body of water where no one is swimming (no humans, anyway—it's hard to avoid fish), limber up the fingers on your throwing hand and get ready to rock 'n' skip.

Find a flat, smooth rock no bigger than your palm. The idea is to hit the water with the flat edge of the rock so that it skims the surface, skipping a few times before sinking.

When you throw the rock, don't throw it overhand or it will sink right away. To make the flat edge hit the water, you've got to throw the rock sidearm.

Hold the rock in your hand so that the flat part is facing the ground. With your arm about waist-high, throw the rock with a sideways sweep. Flick your wrist as you release the rock.

Don't worry if you can't get it on the first few tries—it may take some practice to get the throw right.

How many times can you get your rock to skip?

# #279. Be a DOORKID

The people in uniforms who open doors for others at some hotels and apartment buildings are called doormen.

They also help people carry groceries, hail cabs, announce visitors, accept packages, and do other helpful things for the folks who live or work in the building. It's an old-fashioned custom that has not gone out of style.

You don't need a job at a fancy hotel or high-rise apartment building to act like a doorman. You can offer your services as a doorkid for free.

Pick a local establishment (a store, library, or restaurant) and play doorkid for a while by opening the door for anyone who wants to come in. Ask permission from the owner first, although it's very unlikely anyone would have a problem with such a kind gesture.

Just stand there and open the door for people as they come and go. You'll have a great chance to observe human nature and behavior. Most people will thank you, but a few might look confused—they're not used to nice things like this! You might even earn a few tips!

# #280. JOIN a Fan Club

Do your friends and family get tired of hearing you talk on and on about your favorite TV show, sports team, or music group? Then get together with other people who share your passion—join a fan club.

Most actors, athletes, and musicians have at least one fan club. A lot of fan clubs also have Web sites, so try searching online. At the library or bookstore you can also check out books that list fan clubs. Many celebrity biographies offer the fan-club information, and musicians often include it in their album's liner notes.

While some celebrities have an official fan club, they may also have any number of unauthorized clubs, run by fans just like you. If your favorite star doesn't have a fan club, start one yourself. You can create a Web site and send out a newsletter to your fellow fans.

Fan-club members share news, exchange stories about their star, swap photos, and so on. They often produce a newsletter (print or e-mail). There are no rules. Show your appreciation and enjoy one another's company any way that works for you.

# #281. LEARN Ten Constellations

Thousands of years ago, ancient astronomers grouped the stars into connect-the-dot shapes and pictures to make sense of the twinkling lights above their heads.

Find ten constellations in the sky and learn the stories behind the stars. Check out a sky chart at your library—the stars look different from different locations and at different times of the year.

The constellations were named for mythological beings, characters in stories, animals, people, and objects. Today, there are eighty-eight different constellations, twelve of which make up the signs of the zodiac.

One constellation to find is the Big Dipper—it looks like a saucepan. The Big Dipper is part of a larger constellation called Ursa Major, or the Big Bear. The Dipper's handle is the bear's tail, while the pot is the bear's back.

### Here are a few more constellations to try to find in the night sky:

| | | |
|---|---|---|
| Andromeda | Hercules | Libra |
| Pegasus | Gemini | Pleiades |
| Orion | Hydra | Cassiopeia |

# #282. DESIGN Money

In the late 1990s, in an effort to reduce counterfeiting, the U.S. Treasury began redesigning paper money.

New hundred-, fifty-, twenty-, ten-, and five-dollar bills are now in circulation. The new bills feature larger, more detailed portraits (the more details there are, the harder it is to copy), as well as a special watermark that is applied when the paper is made.

How would you have redesigned the bills? Sketch out how you'd like a new one-dollar bill to look. It can be a variation on how our currency looks now, or it can be completely different—new colors, shapes, emblems, and even a new portrait.

It is quite an honor to be pictured on money. But George Washington (the one-dollar bill), Abraham Lincoln (the five-dollar bill), Alexander Hamilton (the ten-dollar bill), Andrew Jackson (the twenty-dollar bill), Ulysses S. Grant (the fifty-dollar bill), and Benjamin Franklin (the hundred-dollar bill) never knew the honor, because bills didn't appear until after their deaths.

To learn more about money and how it's printed check out www.bep.treas.gov.

# #283. LISTEN to a Worm Walk

You've probably never thought about a worm taking steps. That's because a worm's feet, called setae, are so tiny, you've probably never noticed them before.

Worms move themselves through the dirt using hundreds of these setae, located underneath their bodies. You can listen to an earthworm walking by placing it on a piece of sandpaper. Make sure you listen closely—tiny feet make tiny sounds! If your worm doesn't move, place the paper in a brightly lit spot and the worm will start to wiggle around in search of shade.

If you run your fingers along the underside of the worm, you can feel the setae. Each segment of the worm has four pairs of feet. To get a closer look, use a magnifying glass.

Can you imagine having hundreds of feet? That's a whole lot of shoes to buy!

# #284. FORM Famous Structures

You, too, can be the Washington Monument, the Lincoln Memorial, the Eiffel Tower, or even the Hoover Dam.

With a group of friends, make a list of famous structures around the world that you could imitate simply by twisting, bending, stretching, or otherwise changing your body shape. Take a look at some photos of the world's most well-known buildings, monuments, and landmarks and figure out how you could simulate them with your bodies.

The Washington Monument is one of the easiest ones—you can do it alone, actually. Just stand with your arms stretched straight up above your head, touching the tips of your fingers in a point. The Lincoln Memorial is a little more involved. You'll need to cast some friends as columns surrounding the actual statue, one lucky friend as Lincoln's chair, and another as the president himself.

A few more to try are Stonehenge, Mount Rushmore, and the Great Wall of China. Can you think of others? Which one is the most challenging?

# #285. SAY "HELLO" in Five Languages

Learn to greet people from Tokyo to Tel Aviv to Texas—in their own language.

Even if you aren't going anywhere, you never know when you might meet someone from another country. Here are a few ways to say "hello":

Spanish: hola (OH-la)
Swahili: jambo (JAHM-boh)
Japanese: konnichiwa (koh-NEE-chee-wah)
Hebrew: shalom (sha-LOHM)
Russian: zdravstvujtye (zdrah-stvooy-tee)

# #286. SAY "THANK YOU" in Five Languages

The words *thank you* are powerful, and they can get you pretty far in a foreign country. To start you off, here it is in five languages:

Spanish: gracias (GRAH-see-us)
Swahili: asante asana (ah-SAN-tay ah-SA-na)
Japanese: arigatō (ah-ree-GAH-tow)
Hebrew: toda (to-DA)
Russian: spasibo (spah-SEE-bow)

# #287. INVENT a Secret Code

Keep your letters, notes, and e-mails completely private by writing them in a secret code that only you and your friends can decipher.

There are lots of ways to create a secret code. You can jumble up the letters of the alphabet. For instance, make A=B, B=C, and so on. Or you can mix up the letters even more; for example, make A=F, B=R, and so on. Make sure every letter is assigned only once. The more jumbling you do, the harder it will be for anyone to crack your code, but it will also be harder for you to remember what each letter really stands for!

You can also use pictures or symbols to stand for each letter. You could use an eye for A, a star for B, a hammer for C, and so on. Or try substituting punctuation symbols for each letter. Then you can use letters as punctuation marks.

Write a message in your secret code and see if your friend can decipher it without a clue. Then teach him or her your code so that you have someone to write to!

# #288. GO Sled Bowling

Sled bowling has all the fun of regular bowling, but with less noise (and no funny shoes).

After a snowstorm, get out your sled and head to the nearest hill for a little game of sled bowling. At the bottom of the hill, make snow pins—bowling pins out of snow. Set up ten pins in a cluster right in the path of the oncoming sleds.

The bowling ball is you, hurtling down the hill on your sled straight for the pins. Before you start down the hill, though, make sure there are no rocks or other obstacles in your path (including other sledders!). If you knock down all ten of your pins, you've hit a strike! If some pins are left standing, head back up the hill and try again to hit the remaining pins for a spare.

Take turns with friends hitting the pins and building new ones. You can even team up and play against one another.

The only problem with sled bowling is that there's no conveyor belt (or ski lift) to automatically return you and your sled to the top of the hill.

# #289. Do the LIMBO

How low can you go?

The limbo is a West Indian dance in which people pass under a horizontal pole or stick while bending over backward. The dance gets harder and harder to do because the stick gets lowered slightly after each round. To make it under the limbo stick, you have to bend farther and farther backward in each successive round. As the dance gets more difficult, it gets more fun to watch.

Ask two people to hold either end of a stick, making sure it's always parallel to the ground and it stays steady, as one by one the dancers creep under it, while lively music plays in the background. If someone touches the stick, falls, puts a hand down on the ground, or bends forward, he or she is out. The last person left dancing is the winner!

To be a great limbo dancer you've got to be very flexible. Some limbo champions can make it under when the stick is only a few inches off the ground!

# #290. CALCULATE with Crickets

Male crickets make chirping sounds to serenade females. They do this by rubbing their legs or wings together. The warmer the air temperature is, the more chirping the crickets do.

You can use this fact to calculate the air temperature. Choose a warm summer night to conduct your test—crickets come out in full force when it's hot out. Make sure you bring a watch, because you'll need to count the number of cricket chirps you hear in fifteen seconds. Bring a pal along, too, and one of you can count cricket chirps while the other watches the clock. Add thirty-seven to the number of chirps you hear in fifteen seconds, and that gives you the temperature in degrees Fahrenheit.

Even though the frequency of cricket chirping is different from species to species, the number you calculate will be pretty close to the right temperature.

While male crickets sing their songs, female crickets keep silent, listening with ears located close to their knees!

# #291. BE a Plant-Sitter

Plant-sitting isn't sitting on top of plants; it's taking care of other people's greens while they are away.

Since most houseplants need to be watered a few times a week, if their owners are gone for an extended period of time, the plants will get pretty thirsty and might even die. So the next time someone you know is going away for more than a week, offer to be a plant-sitter for their green companions.

Arrange either to take their plants over to your house or to have them leave you a key so you can let yourself in to tend to the greenery. The plant owner will let you know how much water each plant needs and how often it should be watered.

Some people even believe that talking to plants is good for them. So be sure to talk to the plants you're sitting for—they'll be lonely without anyone else in the house. No one is claiming that a plant is much of a conversationalist, but no one says a heart-to-heart has to go both ways, anyway.

# #292. ATTRACT a Spider

Want to see a spider up close and personal? Send out the right vibes and you could convince one to come out and see you some time.

Because they eat so many creepy-crawly pests, spiders are very helpful to humans. Follow these instructions to attract a spider with sound.

To make spider-friendly music, you'll need a tuning fork, preferably one that vibrates about two hundred times a second. If you don't have a tuning fork, see if you can borrow one from your music or science teacher. Hold the fork by its handle and knock it against a hard surface. Then gently hold one of its prongs against the web and see what happens. The sweet sounds should send the spider running over to the fork!

The spider responds to the tuning-fork's activity because it is very tuned in to the web's movement. It has specialized receptors in its eight legs, allowing it to tell from the vibration of its web what kind of prey is trapped. Spiders don't get caught in their own webs because they know which strands are sticky and which ones aren't.

# #293. BREAK Your Own Record

Beating a world record is one thing, but overcoming a personal record can be even more challenging, and also more rewarding.

How many times in a row can you bounce a ball on your knee? How fast can you run across a football field? How many push-ups can you do? How many cartwheels can you do in a row?

Try a few activities like these and write down each of your records. Then try to beat each one. You'll find that some records (like bouncing a ball on your knee) are just a matter of luck and concentration, while other records (like sit-ups and running) will take practice and time to beat.

Besides physical goals, you can also set personal improvement goals. Try to beat the number of As you received on your last report card, or see how many days you can go without watching TV or eating junk food. Find out how many books you can read in a month and try to top the record!

No matter what kind of personal record you break, reward yourself when you do.

# #294. MAKE a Rain Stick

During the next heat wave, go outside and play a rain stick at the sky to remind the clouds to open up and pour rain on the parched Earth.

The people who live in the rain forests of South America play rain sticks to remind the gods to bring rain to the Earth. Traditional rain sticks are made from dried cactus. Thorns are pressed into the hollow cactus branch, and when pebbles fall over the thorns, it sounds like rain falling through the trees.

Instead of thorns, press thirty straight pins into the inside of a cardboard tube (from a roll of paper towels or wrapping paper) in five rows of six pins each. Put a piece of tape around each row to keep the pins in place. Tape one end of the tube shut, and carefully pour in a handful of pebbles (seeds, small shells, or uncooked rice also work well). Then tape the other end shut. You can cover your rain stick with paper and decorate it with markers, paint, and feathers.

This old phrase will amuse your parents. Tell them you're prepared to sing for your supper, and the supper they make must be as good as the song.

Singing takes talent, and making a good dinner does, too, so it seems like a fair trade. Even if your parents regularly make good dinners, this could raise the stakes.

Give your singing performance a day before the dinner, not five minutes before your usual dinnertime. That gives your personal chefs time to prepare a meal based on how well you sang.

But remember, this is subjective. That means it's your parents' opinion that will determine how well you'll eat. They are not obligated to like your rendition just because they love you. (And if they don't like it, they'll still love you!)

Once you're done singing, don't ask how you did, and tell them not to share their reaction. Wait until the food is on the table. You'll see for yourself in no time just how impressive you were. All those rehearsals in the bath or shower just might have paid off.

# #296. VISIT a Lighthouse

The world's first lighthouse was built in Alexandria, Egypt, in 280 BCE. Standing over 380 feet tall, it was the tallest building in the world.

The first open-sea lighthouse (built on an island or other small, rocky point off the mainland) was built in France in 1611. In 1716 the first lighthouse in the American colonies was built in Boston Harbor.

Lighthouses sit upon the shorelines shining their bright lights and sounding their foghorns to warn ships at sea how close they are to land.

Today there are many lighthouses to explore, some still in operation. A lot of them have tours, and if not, all lighthouses can be appreciated from the outside. To find a lighthouse near you, check out the library or visit these two Web sites: www.cr.nps.gov/maritime/maripark.html and www.lighthousegetaway.com. You can even stay overnight in some lighthouses, although you may have to help the lighthouse keeper with his chores. Check out www.lighthouse.cc/links/overnight.html to find an accommodating lighthouse.

# #297. HAVE a LUAU at Home

One of the world's best parties is the luau, a Hawaiian extravaganza thrown to honor leaders or to mark special occasions such as weddings.

The festivities include nonstop music, dancing, singing, and plenty of food, including the famous roasted pig and poi, a paste made from the ground root of a taro plant. Throw a luau in your own backyard, any time of year, pig or no pig.

Make your own leis with string and fresh flowers or leaves. With an adult's help, light torches or lanterns around the yard, to keep bugs away and for decoration. They are available at many discount department stores.

Ask guests to wear Hawaiian shirts, grass skirts, and flowers in their hair, and to arrive just before sunset. Adorn every guest with a lei as he or she arrives. Keep Hawaiian music—available in any music store—playing all night. Anyone play the ukulele? If so, give him or her center stage!

Most important, make sure no one leaves before dancing the hula.

# #298. MAKE a Snow Sculpture

Newly fallen snow is easy to sculpt. It's sticky, pliable, and packs hard—especially if you add a little cold water to it. Grab a handful and create your own frosty masterpiece!

The next snow day you have off from school, hold your own art class right in your backyard. Create a snow sculpture out of winter's modeling clay—fresh, wet snow. What will you sculpt? A frosty flower? An icy iguana? A snowy serpent?

Roll large snowballs together to make the base. Now form the rough shape of your sculpture, and then use a blunt tool like a shovel, spoon, or butter knife to add detail. To add a splash of color, fill a spray bottle with water and add a few drops of food coloring. Then bring your design to life by spritzing it with colored water.

You might not be the only snow sculptor in your neighborhood. Organize an art show so that all the kids on your block can show off their snowy creations!

# #299. LOOK for Lost Change

Every desk, shelf, and couch in your house could be a treasure trove of lost change; you've just got to dig a little deeper to find it.

Little things like coins often fall behind, into, or underneath furniture, and they remain there, unknown and forgotten, until you rearrange the room.

Don't wait for moving day to sponsor an excavation. Spend some time exploring the dark and cobwebby crevices of your house, looking for lost change. You might not find much more than dust bunnies, but it is possible to amass a small fortune in change and the occasional bill, too.

You can also expect to uncover a paper clip or two, some crumbs, a pen here and there, possibly a button, and maybe even something you didn't know you were missing. (Be prepared in case you stumble across things you don't want to find, such as a dead fly. It happens.)

If your parents know you're doing this, they might ask you to kill two birds with one stone and clean, too. You may not feel *that* adventurous....

# #300. HOLD a No-Laughing Contest

Do we consciously choose to laugh, or does it just happen uncontrollably when we see something funny?

That's a hard question. Scientists have not found a conclusive biological reason why humans laugh, although many people think it's because laughing makes us feel good and therefore helps keep us healthy.

Most of the time we can count on our friends to make us laugh. But see if you have the power to resist, just once. To make things even more challenging, face off against your funniest friend.

Stare at your friend while he or she tries to make you laugh. Your friend can do anything except touch you (no tickling!). Although you can crack a smile, you absolutely cannot laugh. When you do, you're out. How long does it take for you to break up?

Then switch, and see if you can make your friend laugh in even less time. You can also team up against another pair, but both members must laugh to be out.

If someone laughs so hard that milk shoots out of his or her nose, you're Laughmaker-of-the-Year.

Have you ever slept under a buffalo's hide?

Many Plains Native American tribes were nomadic, following buffalo or other sources of food across the North American grasslands. These tribes—like the Blackfoot and the Dakota—lived in tepees. These easily transportable forms of shelter were cone-shaped tents made of poles and animal skins.

To build a tepee, you'll need poles and a tarp (a blanket will also work, but only if the weather cooperates). Mark a circle on the ground where you'd like to build your tepee. Spread your poles out evenly around the circle and drive the lower ends into the ground.

Position the poles so that they aim upward toward a central point. If you can, try to leave an open space at the top—this is how Native Americans let smoke from cooking fires escape from inside. Cover the structure with the tarp or blanket, starting at one stake and wrapping it around the whole structure. Huddle inside, and imagine what it was like to be a buffalo hunter living on the Great Plains centuries ago.

Just because they are small and creepy doesn't mean bugs and spiders deserve to die. The next time you find a crawling creature in your house, don't squish it—rescue it!

Do you remember how small and frightened Jack felt after he climbed the beanstalk and found himself in the giant's castle? That's probably how a spider, fly, or other bug feels inside your house. They don't mean to frighten or annoy anyone—they probably came in by accident and want only to get out.

Don't swat them or stomp them. Show a little compassion for your insect and spider guests by kindly showing them the door.

When you spot a spider or insect in your house, try to capture it with a paper cup and a thin piece of cardboard. Carefully cover the critter with the cup and slide the cardboard under the opening, so it can't escape. Scurry to the door or window and set your unwanted guest free.

You'll be a hero to bugs everywhere.

# #303. SEND a Secret Message

You don't have to be a spy or own fancy gadgets to send your own top secret messages.

Do you have something important to write—a diary entry, the directions to a surprise party, or a secret story—but you don't want anyone to accidentally read it? Then write it in invisible ink!

Here's what you do. Take a lemon and cut it in half. Then squeeze the juice from both halves of the lemon into a bowl. Find a cotton swab or a felt-tip pen that's out of ink and dip it into the lemon juice. Now write your secret message on a piece of paper with the juice-soaked cotton swab or felt-tip pen. When it's time for your message to be revealed, ask an adult to help you use a hot iron to press down on the paper. Then voila—the words will appear before your eyes!

# #304. CREATE Your Own Jigsaw Puzzle

Create your very own jigsaw puzzle in a few simple steps. First, choose a picture that you like from a calendar, magazine, poster, or photograph (always check with your family first to make sure the picture is okay to use). To make an even more personalized puzzle, draw or paint the picture yourself.

After you've chosen your picture, cut it out and glue it onto a piece of cardboard. Wait until the glue dries, then cover the picture with a clear acrylic coating to protect it. You can find acrylic in art supply stores. Let the acrylic dry, then take a pair of scissors and cut the cardboard into pieces. Before you cut, you might want to draw in pencil on the back of the puzzle the sizes and shapes of the pieces you'd like. And remember, the more pieces you cut out, the harder the puzzle will be!

Do you have friends or relatives who are also puzzle lovers? You can give them your puzzles as gifts.

# #305. MIX UP Your Meals

It's always the same: breakfast at 8 AM, lunch at 12 noon, and dinner at 6 PM. Put some dazzle into your eating schedule—mix up your family's mealtimes.

Eating the same kinds of food at the same times every day can get pretty boring. Instead of eating pork chops and mashed potatoes for dinner at 6 PM, try having them for breakfast instead. Or fix pancakes with bacon and orange juice for lunch one day. Instead of scarfing down your bologna sandwich at noon, have your sandwich at dinnertime.

You can mix up your family's meals even more. Instead of eating in the early evening, plan a late-night supper that you eat at the stroke of midnight. With your parents' permission, on a Friday or Saturday night (or any other nonschool night), celebrate the passing of one day into the next with a midnight feast. If it's warm outside, make the feast into a moonlit midnight picnic. Spread a blanket on your lawn and enjoy your food under the stars.

You'll find those mixed-up meals taste delicious!

# #306. SIMULATE the Lunar Landscape

Traveling into space might be a common way to vacation by the time you grow up. Why wait? Bring a little piece of the moon here to Earth.

With some friends, find a patch of dirt or sand somewhere in your neighborhood that has no vegetation (no grass, trees, flowers, bushes, weeds, or even dry leaves) and no trace of human or animal life (no house, car, trash, signs, or footprints). Maybe there are lots where houses have not been built yet, maybe there's a spot in the woods, or maybe you live near a beach. Don't trespass, though—ask an adult if it's okay to be there.

Place a few rocks about. Plant a U.S. flag the way the astronauts did. *Don't* try to dig huge moon craters!

If possible, take black-and-white photographs of your lunar landscape, making sure there's no earthly evidence, such as trees or houses, in the background.

To make the setting complete, you must, of course, walk slowly and in an exaggerated manner, as every serious astronaut impersonator does.

# #307. TRACE Your Family Tree

Do you ever look at your family and wonder, "Where did these people come from?" Trace your family tree!

Write your name at the bottom of a piece of paper. Write your siblings' names next to yours on the same line. Then write your parents' full names on the line above yours. Now draw a line between your parents. From that line, draw a line down to you and to each of your siblings.

Write your aunts' and uncles' full names next to your dad or mom, depending on whose brother or sister they are. Put your mom's parents above her name, and your dad's parents above his. Draw a line between your mom's parents, and from that line draw a line to your mom and her siblings. Do this for your dad's side, too. Repeat for as far back as you want to (or are able to) go.

Some family trees include pictures of each person as well. Ask your parents if they have any old pictures lying around.

Have you ever bought something you've been saving up for and found you didn't get what you paid for?

Writing a letter of complaint is an effective way of voicing your dissatisfaction—and getting results. It is best to type the letter so it is easily legible. Include your address and the date, the name and address of the person or company to whom you are sending the letter. Clearly state your complaint, including brief details and what compensation you would like. Conclude by thanking the person for reading your complaint, and sign the letter. Send a copy to your local Better Business Bureau for even better results.

123 Strawberry Street
Cherrytown, TX 12345
June 20

Bears Galore
1 Teddy Street
Bearsville, CT 54321

Dear Sir or Madam,
I sent away for your giant Ted D. Bear. Your catalog said it was life-size, but when I opened the package, I found it was only 3 inches tall. I would like my money back as soon as possible. Thank you.

Sincerely yours,
Jessica Berry

# #309. RUN a Lemonade Stand

Everyone knows that nothing tastes better on a hot summer day than a glass of sweet, cold lemonade. So give the people what they want!

On a sweltering day, set up a lemonade stand and watch the money start rolling in. Get a small table and chair, some paper cups, a small garbage can, and a change box and set up your refreshment stand on the sidewalk of a well-traveled street. Tip: Set up your stand on the sunny side of the street. People are thirstier in the sun than they are in the shade.

Lemonade is the old standby offering, but you can sell any refreshing drink such as fruit punch or iced tea—as long as it's cold. Check with local delis and fast-food restaurants to find out the going rate for a cold drink about the same size as the one you're offering. Then sell your lemonade cheaper to beat the competition.

# #310. SWITCH Places with a Friend

If imitation is the sincerest form of flattery, you and a friend will be flattering each other all day long.

Choose one of your best friends and switch places with each other for an entire day. Wear each other's clothes (if you wear glasses, keep your own glasses, though!), spend time with each other's family, walk and talk like each other, even eat the food that the other person loves to eat. If your friend loves bananas, then eat a banana that day.

Watch the same TV shows that your friend likes. If your friend is in the middle of reading a book, pick up where he or she left off. Later in the day, get together while still acting like the other person.

Since your families will have to go along with you, be sure to check with your parents first. Your teachers won't appreciate your friend turning in your homework and vice versa, so it's best to do this on a Saturday or during the summer. And don't switch places on the day your family leaves for vacation—you'll be left behind!

# #311. LEARN Birdcalls

Listen to the chirps and chatter of various birds online or on CDs from the library. You just might hear one or two familiar voices that make you say, "So that's who's waking me up every morning!"

Here are a few birdcalls to get you started:

American robin: "tserp tserp tserp"
black-capped chickadee: "chick-a-dee-dee"
blue jay: "choo-a choo-a"
house finch: "tweet"

# #312. FEED the Birds

Create a treat that no feathered friend will be able to resist!

Get four apples and spread peanut butter over them. Pour birdseed (available at pet stores and some grocery stores) into a small bowl and roll the apples around in it until they are completely covered.

Place the seed-covered apples in the crooks of a tree. Be sure the apples are well balanced so that they don't fall when a bird comes by for a nibble.

# #313. MAKE a House of Mirrors

Make a house of mirrors and you'll be seeing double!

You don't need to go to an amusement park for thrills. You can turn your own house into a hilarious attraction! To make a house of mirrors, look around your home for any mirrors that you can move easily. If you don't have many mirrors around the house, you can find some pretty inexpensive ones at the hardware store. Cheap mirrors offer a special bonus because they often will distort, which will make your house of mirrors extra frightening!

Check with your parents first to make sure it's okay; then pick a room to set up the house of mirrors in. Line up the mirrors in a circle, or along a path that winds through the room. Be creative with your setup! Play scary music in the background. Is it scarier with the lights on or off?

Invite your friends over and send them through the house of mirrors. If you really want to give them a good scare, hide behind one of the mirrors and jump out at them!

# #314. VOLUNTEER at an Animal Shelter

If you love animals and have some extra time on your hands, donate it to your local animal shelter.

Just about every community has an animal protection agency or humane society that runs a shelter for abandoned, abused, and unwanted pets. The shelter finds loving homes for these animals through free adoption.

Shelters are always looking for volunteers to help care for the many dogs, cats, and other animals they have waiting for adoption. You can walk the dogs, help give the animals baths, or just spend time petting and playing with them. If you are allergic to animals, you can still help out. The shelter may need help in the office, stuffing envelopes or making phone calls.

Visit the ASPCA (American Society for the Prevention of Cruelty to Animals) Web site at www.aspca.org to find a shelter near you. If your family is thinking about getting a pet, consider adopting one from a shelter. You'll make a loving pet very happy.

# #315. LOOK for Lost Civilizations

Don't be quick to say that there are no lost civilizations near you ... if you knew about them, they wouldn't be lost, would they?

Okay, the reality is there probably aren't any, unless you happen to live in the heart of the jungle. But look anyway.

As long as you ask an adult for permission and go with a group, explore the woods or desert nearest your house. Pretend you're really on the trail of a legendary city that vanished thousands of years ago . . . by earthquake . . . or volcano . . . or tidal wave . . . or . . . ?

Look for signs such as buried objects, markings on trees or stones, or strange clearings. As you search, *create* what you're searching for.

Then take your search to the library, where you can read about lost or unexplained civilizations such as the supposed sinking of Atlantis and Easter Island (the one with the big stone heads, called Moai.)

You should *never* stop looking for that fabled civilization, no matter how old you get.

# #316. Have an ART Exhibit

Isn't it time you got credit for your hard work in art class? Have an art exhibit!

Ask your friends to choose three to five of their favorite pieces of artwork and to bring them to your house. The works can be anything from collages to drawings to ceramic statues. Make a catalog of all the art that you'll be showing, and be sure to include the title of the piece and the artist's name.

On the day before the show, set up all of the artwork around your house. Place the pieces on tables, chairs, or hang them on walls. Use index cards as nameplates for each piece so that guests know who each artist is. Write down the title, artist, and year it was created, and mount each card next to the corresponding work.

Make sure that all of the artists are at your house on the day of the show. That way they'll be around to answer any of the guests' questions. Show people around the display, and smile as people compliment you on all of your hard work!

# #317. TIE-DYE a T-Shirt

Tired of boring white T-shirts? Take your old shirt and give it a makeover!

Tie-dying is an easy way to give your clothes some zip. First, buy fabric dyes and put each different color into a separate bowl. Next, take a plain white T-shirt, twist parts of it or tie some knots and secure them with rubber bands.

If you want the T-shirt to be a single color, soak the whole shirt in one of the bowls for the amount of time indicated on the package of fabric dye. If you want a multicolored T-shirt, dip different parts of the shirt into different bowls, allowing the shirt to soak in each color. After you've finished dying the shirt, remove it from the bowl and dip it in water until all the excess color is rinsed off. Take off the rubber bands, untie the knots, and hang the shirt up to dry. Now your shirt is a work of art!

You don't have to limit yourself to T-shirts. Use your imagination—how about tie-dyed socks or tie-dyed beach towels?

# #318. FORM a Barbershop Quartet

They don't have Top 40 hits. They aren't in heavy rotation on the music video channels. They don't sell out stadiums. But barbershop quartets still sound good.

The first barbershop quartets were groups of four singers who used to sing harmony in—you guessed it—barbershops. The trend began in the late 1800s and continued into the twentieth century. Although they don't sing in barbershops anymore, barbershop quartets are still harmonizing all across the country.

Barbershop singing has had a bunch of musical influences, including African-American soul music and European hymns. Quartets sing without any accompaniment in close harmonies. They are great to listen to and even more fun to sing with. Find a barbershop group near you or form a quartet of your own and begin belting out barbershop tunes.

A great place to start your search is with the Barbershop Harmony Society at www.barbershop.org. There you'll learn all about how to sing in a barbershop quartet, where you can listen to one, and how you can join a group near you.

# #319. INVENT a New Sport

The playing fields, tracks, and pools are jam-packed with all different kinds of sports, anything from Roller Derby to water polo, but there is always room for more.

Sports have been popular with people since ancient times. Every four years, the ancient Greeks held their Olympic Games in which athletes competed in wrestling, racing, weight lifting, discus throwing, and more. The Romans watched sporting events in the Colosseum.

Although baseball and basketball seem as though they have been around forever, they are relatively new sports. The first game of baseball was played on June 19, 1846, in Hoboken, New Jersey, while basketball was invented in 1891 by a Massachusetts gym teacher.

Invent a new sport for the twenty-first century. The possibilities are endless. Your sport can involve a bat, a ball, nets, even spoons, pieces of cardboard, and a balloon—whatever you want! It can be played on a field, a court, a rink, or in a pool. You can play one-against-one or in teams. Whatever sport you invent, teach the rules to a bunch of friends, and let the games begin!

# #320. LIST the Seven Wonders of Your Town

There were Seven Wonders of the Ancient World and there are seven wonders of the natural world. What are the seven wonders of your town?

The world is full of wonders, but the Seven Wonders of the World are what many people think are the most wonderful. Of the Seven Wonders of the Ancient World, only one is left standing—the Pyramids of Egypt. Others included the Pharos (Lighthouse) of Alexandria and the Hanging Gardens of Babylon. The seven wonders of the natural world include the Grand Canyon in Arizona, Mount Everest in Nepal, and the Great Barrier Reef in Australia.

If you were to list the seven wonders of your own town, what would they be? What are the most spectacular buildings, houses, or natural landmarks? List anything that is unique or special about your town. Maybe the ultra-nice people are one of your town's wonders? Or perhaps a teacher who has taught since your parents went to school? Or maybe the championship-winning marching band?

# #321. DRESS from Another Decade

Did you ever look at photos of your parents when they were your age and think, "What on earth were they wearing?"

Fashions change with the times, and some come in and out of style. Do you have a thing for poodle skirts and saddle shoes from the 1950s? Or do you go more for the tie-dye T-shirts and love beads from the 1960s? Maybe you like the bell-bottom hip-hugging jeans and polyester pantsuits from the 1970s? Or even the neon colors and miniskirts of the 1980s?

Whatever your fashion passion, spend a day dressed from a decade other than your own. Raid your parents' closet to see if they have any fashion relics from times gone by. Or you can check out thrift stores and Salvation Army shops for used (and inexpensive!) clothes from other eras.

If you're not sure how they dressed in the past, go to the library and look at the fashion magazines from the decade of your choice. You might even notice that while most of the styles are not stylish anymore, some trends from the past may have made a comeback.

# #322. TAKE Underwater Photos

The first disposable cameras were introduced in 1986. The cameras *are* the film—when the roll is done, you take the whole plastic contraption to be processed and get only photos back (the camera is used up).

An underwater disposable camera is the same thing except it's coated with a clear plastic shell. They are designed for taking photos in shallow depths.

Many places that sell regular disposable cameras also carry underwater disposables, especially in the summer.

If you have access to a pool, buy an underwater camera and arrange a wacky photo shoot. Get old clothes—that's right, clothes—such as shirts and ties. Dress up and dive in! Underwater photos are wild on their own, but even more hysterical if you're dressed!

Of course, feel free to take pictures wearing regular bathing suits, too. Vary the poses. Reenact scenes from history, books, or movies, and take group shots.

Remember that underwater, nobody can hear you say "Cheese."

# #323. Go on a SCAVENGER HUNT

A scavenger hunt is a great way to really get to know your neighborhood (and possibly your neighbors).

Along with a few friends, come up with a list of about ten items that can be found near where you live. What you put on the list is entirely up to you as long as the objects (a) aren't stolen and (b) are small enough to carry (no boulders!). Here are a few suggestions: a black pen, an egg, a take-out menu, an autograph from a cashier at the grocery store, a quarter from the 1980s.

You can also limit your search to your backyard and include things like a garden tool, a maple tree leaf, a white rock, etc. Or you can create your list around themes: red things (rose, lipstick, tomato), or the alphabet (everyone finds something that starts with every letter of the alphabet).

Once you have your list, split your group into teams and set off in search of your items. The first team to gather everything on the list wins.

## #324. INVENT a Stew

Let's face it, when it comes to stews, what else can you say except "Been there, done that"? Get out of the dinner doldrums with a fantastic stew concoction of your own.

A stew is basically a really thick soup in which all the ingredients are thrown together in a big pot and cooked for a while over the stove. Most stews include some sort of broth, water, or milk (to make it soupy) as well as vegetables and/or meat.

Check out a stew recipe in a cookbook. You can replace the vegetables and meat suggested by the recipe with the vegetables and meat you want to use instead. If you hate broccoli, don't use it; this is your stew. If you are using meat, make sure it gets cooked all the way through, or better yet, use precooked meat. Before you start cooking, check with your parents.

When the stew is done, serve it to your family. Your first concoction may not turn out to be delicious. If it isn't, try to figure out what went wrong and fix it the next time. Happy cooking!

# #325. LEARN First Aid

The most important thing to do when someone gets hurt is to remain calm and not to panic. If you get upset and nervous, you'll only make the injured person more agitated, which could harm him or her even more.

There is a lot to learn about first aid, but here are a few basic procedures:

**BLEEDING:** Apply pressure to the wound with a clean cloth; elevate the wound above the heart if possible.

**BURN:** Cover the burn with cold water if the skin is unbroken and there are no blisters. Pat dry and cover with a clean bandage. If the skin is charred, don't do anything and call 911.

**FAINTING:** Lay the victim down on his or her back and raise both legs. Loosen any tight clothing and apply a cool, damp rag to the face. If the victim doesn't become alert after a couple of minutes, or if anything else seems wrong, call 911.

> There is so much to learn about first aid
> that taking a course is a great idea.
> Check with your community center, school, or local
> hospital to find out if they offer courses for kids.

# #326. WRITE the Middle

Most stories have a beginning, a middle, and an end.

Write the missing middles for very different story beginnings and endings. Take the beginning sentence or paragraph from one book or story and the ending from another and write a middle that connects the two.

It's much easier (and far more dull) to choose a beginning and an end from two very similar stories. To make it trickier and much more interesting, choose a beginning and an end from two stories that couldn't be more unlike each other.

For instance, if your beginning sentence or paragraph is about King Arthur's knights, choose an ending about landing on Mars or skiing in the Swiss Alps. You'll have to come up with some exciting plot twists to connect the two themes together in a believable way.

Try doing this with a friend, too. Each of you writes the middle for the same beginning and end. You'll be amazed at how different the stories turn out.

# #327. MAKE a Trauma Doll

Going to the hospital isn't fun for anyone, no matter what their age, but for little kids it can be pretty scary. Make a doll to brighten the spirits of a child about to go into the hospital.

A trauma doll is something that a young patient can hug or talk to when he or she feels alone or frightened. Also, the doctors and nurses can use the doll to explain to the child what is happening with his or her own body.

Your trauma doll doesn't have to be elaborate or fancy—just huggable. It doesn't even have to be human. You can also make a trauma teddy bear, elephant, or even a trauma pillow with an encouraging drawing or saying written on it in fabric markers. Check your local craft store or online sites for easy doll patterns and supplies.

There is probably more than one child who could use a trauma doll, so why not get your whole class, club, or youth group in on the doll making? Your craftiness can help make a child's hospital visit a little less scary.

Thousands of different cases are tried in courts throughout the country each day. They may be tried in local, state, or federal courts.

Almost all jury trials are open to the public. The next time you have a free afternoon, go to your local courthouse and find out what cases are being tried that day. Pick one that interests you and watch our justice system in action.

Who do you think should win the case—the plaintiff or the defendant? Is one side's story more believable than the other's? Does one of the lawyers do a better job convincing you? Do you sympathize more with one side than the other?

Watching a court case in action is one of the most interesting activities you can do for free. Chances are you'll learn something about the American court system.

# #329. READ an Animal's Mind

Although animals can't speak and tell us what they are thinking, we can get a pretty good idea about what's going on in their brains by observing their behavior and coming to conclusions about why they do what they do.

For several days, watch what your pet does. Keep a log of all its significant actions. When does your dog bark? Does it bark for the same reason every time? What is it trying to say to you? Maybe, "Someone is at the door." Or, "I'm hungry." Can you tell which thought is being expressed?

Does your cat get frisky right before it gets fed? Does it meow whenever you approach? It might be harder to read your fish's mind, but give it a try. Maybe it swims to the surface when it sees you coming, or opens and closes its mouth when it's hungry.

If you don't have a pet, try observing wild animals like squirrels or birds in your yard or in the park. What is a squirrel thinking when it sees an acorn? Nuttin'.

# #330. CREATE Your Own Country

Sure, you're proud to be a citizen of our great nation, but imagine what it would be like to live in a country that you created yourself.

First, decide where on the globe your country will be located. Will it be an undiscovered island in the Pacific? A stretch of land between the United States and Canada? A peninsula jutting off the coast of India? Or a volcanic island newly formed in the Atlantic?

Next, choose a name for your nation. You can name it after yourself or someone else, even your dog. What kind of government will your country have? Will it be a democracy where every citizen has a vote, a monarchy with a royal family, or some other form of rule? Establish the five most important laws. Perhaps the government will allow kids to choose their own bedtime?

Draw your country's flag. It doesn't have to be a rectangle like most flags. Make it any shape you like. Don't forget to compose a national anthem and sing it proudly, especially on your country's Independence Day.

# #331. BUILD a Terrarium

With a few everyday items, you can create a small, blooming world in a terrarium!

Fill a large, wide-mouthed glass jar with about ½ inch of gravel (to soak up excess moisture), followed by ½ inch of charcoal (to absorb the acids that plants give off as they grow, since too much acid would be fatal to the plants). Add about 3 inches of damp potting soil. Gather several small plants, such as moss or ferns, including any roots and a bit of soil, from outside. Arrange the plants in the jar in whatever way you think looks best, making sure to bury any roots in the soil. Finally, add some rocks and twigs to make the terrarium look like a natural environment. Replace the jar's lid, and poke four holes in it (ask an adult for help!). This will allow the plants to breathe!

Put the terrarium in a room that gets good exposure to natural light, but make sure it isn't in direct sunlight. Give the terrarium a few teaspoons of water each week and watch your plants grow!

# #332. CELEBRATE an Unsung Hero

People who quietly do good things without thanks or recognition are unsung heroes.

Many unsung heroes do good things for others not because they want praise or to draw attention to themselves. They do good things simply because it's a good thing to do.

Write a letter to the editor of your local newspaper celebrating an unsung hero in your life or in the life of someone you know. Did you have a teacher who was especially patient when you were having trouble at school? Has your grandmother or grandfather done incredible things that you want more people to know about? Maybe your parents, who do so much for you, don't get the thanks and praise they deserve? Your dog or cat may be your unsung hero, too, for always being there for you.

You can also celebrate an unsung hero in your community. Call around to local schools, retirement homes, hospitals, or animal shelters and ask if they can tell you about people who give of themselves without asking anything in return.

# #333. DJ a DANCE

Get together a bunch of your dance-loving friends and hold your own dance-fest in your basement, living room, or backyard. Best of all, you choose the music.

To DJ a dance well, you should play a variety of music. That way everyone will find some music that will compel them to dance up a storm!

You don't need fancy or expensive equipment to hold your dance, just an MP3 player and docking station or a computer. You can even go old school and use CDs and a CD player!

You may not have to DJ during the dance itself. You can make a playlist ahead of time and then to start the party, simply push Play. Try to keep the beat pumping for a while, then go for a slow song or two to break it up. Then back to the fast rhythms! Even if you use a playlist, that doesn't mean you must remain on autopilot. Tell your guests they can make requests, and sneak in as many of them as you can.

# #334. MAKE a Treasure Map

Think you'll never find a treasure map leading to buried booty? Create one yourself!

Your treasure can be anything—a few coins, a valuable trading card, or a stash of candy. Seal your treasure in a treasure chest or a plastic container, and bury or hide it.

Age your map so that it looks old and tattered like a pirate's map. Crumple up a piece of white paper and let it soak in a bowl of cold coffee or tea for a few minutes. Then lift out the paper, carefully uncrumple it, and lay it on paper towels to dry. While the paper is still wet, tear pieces off the edges to make it look even more raggedy.

Once the paper is dry, mark the treasure with an X and draw a path that leads to it. Don't make your map too easy to follow. Give clues, possibly as riddles, but don't give any direct info.

Pass the map to a friend or two and see if they can find your treasure. Make sure you're there when they find it, or you might not get your share of the loot.

# #335. GET a Paper ROUTE

Extra! Extra! Read all about it! Getting a paper route is a great way to earn money.

Newspaper companies hire kids like you (and adults) to get their papers to home subscribers before the morning coffee has even been poured.

Check with your local paper and see if they have any delivery routes available. You'll want a route that's near to where you live, in your own neighborhood, if possible. Every morning the papers will be delivered to you, probably before 6 AM. Then you've got to get them to the subscribers' front doors by 6:30 AM. Every week, or every two weeks, you'll collect money from the subscribers. If you go in person, you might get a tip, too. A portion of the money you collect is yours to keep; the rest you hand over to the newspaper company.

Not only will you be earning extra money, but, because you've gotten up so early, you'll never be late for school again.

# #336. GROW a Sponge Garden

You don't need dirt to make a little garden grow. You can sprout some mustard seeds using just a sponge, water, and some sunshine.

Buy a new sponge and cut it into any shape you like—star, heart, flower, or leave it as a rectangle. Wet the sponge and squeeze out the excess water. The sponge should be damp, not soaking. Place the sponge onto a plate or into a bowl and cover it with mustard seeds (you can buy them at the grocery store in the spice aisle). At night, keep the sponge damp by covering it with plastic wrap. During the day, uncover the sponge and place it in a window so that it gets plenty of sunshine. Be sure to mist the sponge several times a day.

The seeds will soon start to sprout. In about two weeks, your sponge will be a tiny herb garden, covered in mustard sprouts. You can harvest your little crop and use your new herbs in a sandwich or salad.

# #337. WRITE Your Own Fairy Tale

Cinderella marries the prince. Snow White marries the prince. Sleeping Beauty marries the prince. It gets a little boring, doesn't it?

Put a new twist on an old fairy tale. Maybe Cinderella could start her own housecleaning business or Little Red Riding Hood could eat the wolf.

Or write a completely new story with original characters. It can take place "Once upon a time," or you can write a fairy tale for the twenty-first century.

# #338. JUMBLE Fairy Tales

Do all fairy tale characters live in the same fairy tale land?

Look at a list of fairy tales on a table of contents or online and look for tales that could have a connection. For example, perhaps the witch of "Hansel and Gretel" is the same as in "Rapunzel"? Or what if Little Red Riding Hood passed Goldilocks in the woods?

Take any two (or more) fairy tales and combine them in a new, overlapping story. You will create a story that seems both familiar and fresh.

# #339. SEND Postcards to Yourself

If your friends never send you postcards when they go on vacation, don't wait by the mailbox for their notes; send some postcards to yourself.

One of the most common vacation activities might be choosing and writing postcards. A really interesting or picturesque postcard is a great a souvenir!

Next time you see one that you like (even if you're not on vacation!), send it to yourself. What's on your mind that day? Write it down! When it arrives, the postcard will bring you back to how you were feeling when you wrote it. Has a lot changed since that moment? Were you upset about something then that seems much less important now? Writing the postcard might be just what you need to vent your frustration.

Were you in a great mood when you found the postcard? Capture your joy in print. Chances are that when you get the postcard, you will feel happy all over again!

Sending postcards to yourself is also a creative way of leaving reminders for yourself.

# #340. MAKE a Rainbow

You don't need rain to see a rainbow of colors—just make your own prism!

White light, which travels in a straight line, has no color. A prism, a wedge-shaped glass object, separates that light into a rainbow of seven colors, called a spectrum. It works because it bends different colors by different degrees.

Different types of light contain varying amounts of each color. For example, sunlight has equal amounts of each color, while fluorescent light has more blue and yellow.

**All you need to create your own prism is a mirror, a clear glass of water, and a piece of paper.**

1. **Place the mirror in a glass of water at a slant, so that it's facing the sun.**

2. **Hold the paper at an angle in front of the mirror.**

3. **Shift the paper around until the colors show up.**

4. **You've just made your very own rainbow!**

# #341. WEAR a New Hairstyle

Have you always worn your hair in pigtails or parted it on the side? Mix it up a little bit and give yourself a new 'do!

You don't have to make a trip to the barbershop or salon to get a new hairstyle—you don't even need a pair of scissors. All you need is a comb and a little imagination. If you part your hair on the side, try parting it in the middle or on the other side for a change. Brush your bangs away from your face, or slick your hair back with gel. You could even use gel to make your hair stick straight up into the air.

If you have long hair, try leaving it down or putting it up—whatever's new for you. Try three braids instead of the usual one or two, or make tons of tiny braids all over your head. Put your hair in a bun with chopsticks.

How does your new hairstyle make you feel? Do you feel older or younger? Dressed up or casual? Maybe just plain crazy?

# #342. BLOW Bubbles

You don't have to be a little kid to love blowing bubbles.

To make extra-huge bubbles, try this solution: Mix together 4 cups of water, 2 cups of liquid dish detergent, 2 cups of glycerin (you can get this at most drugstores), and 2 teaspoons of corn syrup in a big basin. Bend a wire coat hanger into a neat closed shape like a square or a star. Dunk the hanger into the soapy basin and slowly lift it out. Hold it gently and run forward. Look behind and see the huge bubbles floating along!

Experiment with other objects that you might blow bubbles through—old sunglasses without any lenses, yogurt container lids with the middle cut out, or any other enclosed shape. Cut the bottom out of a plastic water bottle and dip it into the soapy solution. Blow into the top and watch the bubbles fly!

# #343. MAKE Your Own Granola

Granola makes a delicious and good-for-you snack—and it tastes even better when you make it yourself!

Making your own granola is a snap! First preheat the oven to 325°F. For six servings, combine 3 cups of uncooked oats, 1 cup of shredded coconut, and 1 teaspoon of cinnamon in a baking pan and mix well. In a bowl, combine 1 cup of chopped nuts (walnuts, almonds, or pecans, whatever you like), ¼ to ½ cup of honey, 1 teaspoon of vanilla extract, and 2 tablespoons of softened butter. Mix well and then pour over the oat mixture in the pan. Bake for 15 to 30 minutes. Remove from the oven and add raisins or dates. Let the granola cool and then store in an airtight container.

You can vary the recipe according to your tastes—if you don't like coconut, leave it out and add chocolate chips instead. Experiment by adding a little more cinnamon or a little less honey—it's all up to you.

# #344. Ask Tough Questions

Some questions have no easy answers, but don't let that stop you from asking them.

Create a list of some of the toughest questions you can think of about life—especially questions that you have pondered yourself. Create another list of people whose responses you'd be interested in hearing. They don't have to be people you know, but they do have to be people in your community whom you could approach.

### Suggested questions:

- ◎ Why is there war?
- ◎ Do you ever lie?
- ◎ What is the happiest thing you've ever done?
- ◎ What are the most important things in life?
- ◎ What happens when we die?

### People you might want to ask:

- ◎ a priest or minister
- ◎ a rabbi
- ◎ a doctor or nurse
- ◎ a police officer
- ◎ a teacher
- ◎ your parents

# #345. TRIM a Mitten Tree

If you looked into it, you'd be surprised at how many people in your town or community don't have enough money to get their kids mittens in the winter.

During the holiday season, instead of thinking about all the things you might get, think about all the things you could give—to people who need them. Get together with some people at your school or house of worship and set up a mitten tree.

If you tell them you'd like to use it to help others, a local farm or tree seller may donate the tree. Stand the tree up in the lobby of your school or house of worship. Ask people to help trim the tree with donations of new or gently used mittens, scarves, and hats. Once your tree is completely decorated, take a photo of it, and then gather up the trimmings to donate to a local children's organization or welfare office.

Your generosity will not only warm hands; it will also warm hearts.

# #346. READ Lips

We listen with our ears, but we can also listen with our eyes . . . by reading lips.

Many of us read lips all the time without realizing it. If we miss a word or a sound in a conversation, we quickly figure out the missing words by watching the movement of the speaker's mouth. Lipreading is sometimes called speech reading, because clues to what is being said are given not only by the lips but also by the tongue.

Many sounds look the same on our lips, and only about 30 percent of English words can be correctly identified by lipreading.

Soldiers who lost their hearing in World War I were taught to lipread, and many, but not all, deaf people read lips.

Try reading the lips of your friends or family. Wear earplugs and ask your friend or family member to speak to you in a soft voice. Watch his or her lips and try to figure out what he or she is saying. It will be harder to read the lips of someone who is chewing gum or eating, or wearing facial hair.

# #347. SEND an Anonymous Note

Feeling sheepish and shy? Send a note anonymously!

Do you have something nice you'd like to tell somebody, but you're too embarrassed to say it to his or her face? Send that person an anonymous note to let him or her know how you feel. Maybe you want to tell someone that you think she's the best basketball player on the team, or that you love the sketch he made in art class.

Sometimes it's easier to express yourself on paper than in person. Writing a note also gives you the leisure to think through what you want to say.

Putting how you feel down on paper might also give you the courage to express yourself in person. Chances are the person receiving your note will feel flattered that you thought of writing to him or her. If you want to, drop clues about your identity in the note, or just leave the recipient wondering!

# #348. MAKE Coupons

Instead of giving a gift like a book or a tie, give your mom or dad a book of coupons that they can redeem from you! They'll appreciate the homemade quality of the gift, and you'll have fun creating them.

Make a list of things that you can give (or do for) your parents that you'd like to offer on the coupons. What about a whole afternoon of cleaning? Breakfast in bed? A game of basketball? A trip to the movies (on you)? A night of babysitting for your younger siblings? Be creative in thinking up ideas for your coupons. What would make your parents happy? How can you help them relax?

Make double coupons, too, which your mom or dad can combine with another coupon to get two times more of whatever the other coupon offers. Be sure you have enough time to do everything that you offer.

Create the coupons on paper and be sure to color them with markers. Combine all the coupons you made into a book, and decorate it, too!

# #349. ATTEND a Different Religious Service

Freedom of religion includes the freedom to attend religious services of faiths other than your own.

Going to another faith's worship service is a great way to discover the similarities and differences among the many religions in the world. Even within religions there are a variety of sects and groups that worship differently. For instance, within Christianity you'll find Catholics, Baptists, Methodists, Lutherans, Episcopalians, Unitarians, Presbyterians, and more. Within Judaism there are the Orthodox, Conservative, and Reform branches, as well as others.

So take a trip to a synagogue (Jewish), a church (Christian), a mosque (Muslim), a pagoda (Buddhist), a mandira (Hindu), or any other house of worship as long as it isn't your own.

Before you visit, it's a good idea to call ahead to find out what the best time is for visitors. While you are there, always be respectful and quiet—especially when people are praying. Seeing how others worship might give you a new perspective on your own religion.

# #350. Hold a BAKE SALE

If you like baking, turn your hobby into some extra cash for yourself. Showcase your talents by holding a bake sale, and people will be unable to resist your delicious treats.

Make sure you have plenty of time to make all of your treats before the bake sale. If you want the sale to be really big, ask friends to help with the baking.

If you want to hold your bake sale at school, check with your principal first. Or, if it's a nice day, set up a table outside in your neighborhood. Post signs nearby to advertise the sale and draw in the hungry hordes.

The amount you charge for each goody may be based on how much the ingredients cost you or how popular you think the treats will be. The more popular treats can be higher priced. If you still have lots left over near the end of the sale, try lowering your prices.

> **If the bake sale is a big success, you could use your profits to invest in ingredients for a future sale. Pretty soon, you'll have your very own baking business!**

# #351. MAKE a Sundial

Tell the time without looking at your watch!

First, fold a 1 foot by 1 foot piece of heavy paper from corner to corner (so it makes a triangle) and unfold. Next, cut the paper in half along the fold line. You will have two triangles. Fold up a 1-inch flap on one of the short sides of a triangle. Draw a line from the center of a 2 foot by 2 foot square of wood to the middle of one of its sides. Lay the flap of the triangle along the line, with the point in the center of the wood square. Attach the paper to the wood with thumbtacks. The triangle should be standing straight up and down.

Put your sundial on a flat surface outside in the sun. For every hour the sun is out, mark where the triangle's shadow is cast. When you have all of the hours of the day marked, your sundial will tell you the time—at least when it's sunny.

**Be sure to keep your sundial in the same place, facing the same direction, or your reading will be wrong.**

# #352. CREATE a Family Coat of Arms

It's hard to recognize someone if he's covered from head to foot in metal armor! In the Middle Ages, knights wore emblems on coats worn over their armor to let other knights know who they were up against—a medieval ID badge, of sorts.

Each knight had his own coat of arms whose symbols told others what the knight was like. An eagle, for instance, was a sign of courage and nobility, while a unicorn was a sign of faithfulness.

Coats of arms were not attached to a family or a last name, but to an individual. If your family has a coat of arms, it is probably from the earliest known person who shares your last name, whether or not he is an ancestor of yours.

Create a coat of arms for your family. For inspiration, check out books on coats of arms (also called heraldry) at the library. What symbols do you think represent your family?

Wear it with pride the next time you don your armor and head out to joust or slay a dragon.

# #353. TRY a New Sport

Tired of playing the same old sports? Put down that bat and ball and try some new games for a change.

Why not take a whack at water polo, give golf a go, or test out tennis? There are tons of sports out there just waiting for you to come out and play. If you always played team sports, try your hand at more individual games like running, tennis, or golf. If you usually go solo, get into group sports—join a rugby, basketball, or soccer team, among others.

To find a team or instructor near you, check with your town's recreation department or your local YMCA or athletic center. These organizations often organize leagues or offer lessons in all sorts of activities.

If you can't find a team to join or an instructor to teach you, check out a rule book at the library or online. Get together with a group of friends and teach yourselves to play. You can also look for instructional videos at the library or video store.

# #354. Set a GOAL and REACH It

Sir Edmund Hillary and Tenzing Norgay, the first people to reach the top of the world's tallest mountain, didn't achieve this goal on their first try. Even after they failed, Hillary and Norgay kept working toward their goal. Eventually on May 28, 1953, they reached the summit of Mount Everest.

What goals do you have for yourself? Decide on three goals you'd like to achieve, one by the end of this month, one by the end of the year, and one by the end of next year. Then create a plan to work toward achieving them. If your goal is to bike all the way to the top of a steep hill without stopping, first try making it up the hill stopping four times. Once you're able to do that, stop one time fewer every time you go up until you reach the top without stopping at all.

With practice, patience, and perseverance you can work toward any goal—whether it's getting to the top of the hill, making better grades, saving more money, or even climbing to the top of the world's tallest mountain.

# #355. MAKE Shadow Puppets

Cast a shadow on your favorite story or play—act it out in your own shadow puppet theater.

Decide on a play or a story you'd like to dramatize, or act out. For each character in your drama, cut an outline out of heavy paper. Keep the shapes simple. Less complicated shapes make shadows that are easier for your audience to see. Tape each outline to a pencil or craft stick.

To create your stage, drape a sheet over a long stick or rod and hang it between two chairs. This is your screen. Place a box behind the sheet to hide yourself and your hands during the show. Set up a bright lamp behind the sheet and ask your audience to sit in front. Act out your play by holding up your puppets between the lamp and the sheet. The puppets will cast shadows on the screen that your audience can see on the other side. If you move the puppets closer to the screen, their shadows will get smaller, but if you hold them closer to the lamp, they'll cast giant shadows onto your screen.

# #356. MASTER a Magic Trick

Abracadabra! Learn to make quarters disappear, make cards leap to the top of the deck, and pull a scarf out of an empty pocket—it's magic!

Most magic tricks aren't magic at all—they are optical illusions and sleight-of-hand maneuvers. With patience and lots of practice, most people can learn to perform magic. Go to the library or bookstore and check out one of the many books about magic. There are even magic tricks online. Whenever you perform, just remember that a magician never reveals how the trick is done.

Try this magic trick that will prove to your audience that you have eleven, not ten, fingers. Hold up both hands. With your right index finger, count the fingers on your left hand, "One, two, three, four, five." Then count the fingers on your right hand with your left index finger, "Six, seven, eight, nine, ten." Then tell the crowd, "Gosh, I thought there were eleven." With your left index finger count backward on your right hand, "Ten, nine, eight, seven, six, plus five is eleven!" Do this last step pretty quickly. Your audience will be stunned!

# #357. WRITE a Fan Letter

If you like listening to music, reading books, or watching movies, chances are you have a favorite musician, writer, or actor.

Many celebrities get hundreds of thousands of fan letters every year. Other celebrities have smaller followings and don't get bags and bags filled with fan mail each day. These people actually read the letters they receive, and many even write back personally, rather than having people who work for them do it.

Choose an athlete, singer, actor, or writer whom you especially admire, and write that person a letter. Tell him or her a bit about yourself and why you're such a big fan. Be sure to ask for a reply. Lots of stars send the fans who write to them autographed portraits of themselves.

But where do you write to? Most stars don't list their home addresses. If you're writing to an author, write in care of his or her publishing company. For an athlete, write to the team's office. And for a musician, send your letter to the record company. They'll be sure to forward your letter to the celebrity.

# #358. BUILD Miniature Monuments

If you want to see the world but have to be in school tomorrow morning, one way is to make mini-monuments. Using only material already around the house, construct the world's wonders on a tabletop!

The Eiffel Tower . . . a bunch of metal beams . . . can you re-create it with paper clips?

The Washington Monument . . . perhaps you could start with a candle or a bar of soap?

The Great Wall of China . . . do you have the time, patience, and massive amounts of blocks to make a really long model of it across the backyard?

Stonehenge . . . okay, it's just rocks. That's an easy one.

Not all of them must be famous. See if you can make an itsy-bitsy igloo with ice cubes. Getting them to stack will be tricky. They're slippery little fellas.

# #359. LEARN Sign Language

Do you know what it's like to be unable to hear sounds? What if you couldn't hear your parents speak, or your favorite songs on the radio?

Deaf people must rely on their other senses to understand what others are trying to say. Many deaf people use sign language, a system of hand gestures, to "see" what others are saying. Different countries have different sign languages. American Sign Language (ASL) is spoken in the United States and Canada and is the third most-used language in America.

Find out if there's anyplace near where you live that offers classes in sign language. If there are no inexpensive classes around, pick up a book on signing from the library. Pretty soon, you'll be able to communicate in a completely new way!

# #360. MAKE a Lunchtime Surprise

One morning pack a lunch for your mom, dad, or one of your siblings to take to work or school, but don't take requests. What's inside the lunch bag should come as a complete surprise.

Make your mother's favorite sandwich, or pour your father's special soup into a thermos. Surprise your sibling with the candy bar you were saving for yourself. Throw in a few other treats, too—fresh fruit, carrot sticks, nuts, home-baked cookies or brownies, or anything else you know your surprise victim can't resist.

Don't just stop at food, either! Toss in a few jokes, photos, and special notes like, "Have a delicious day" or "Hope you like lunch a bunch." You can even put in a new pen or pencil for your family member to use throughout the rest of the day.

Write "Do Not Open Until Lunch" on the lunch bag and set it out on the kitchen counter for your intended surprise-getter.

# #361. INVENT a New Language

Kiom qureey lyore tiogg?
Translation: Can you read this?

We made up that language. Make up one of your own! Start by listing the fifty most common words you use. Next to each word, write its translation in your new language. Keep adding words to your "dictionary."

Name your language and learn it by heart, then teach it to a friend.

# #362. INVENT Your Own Sign Language

Baseball coaches use their own secret sign language to tell their players what to do. Follow baseball's example and create a secret sign language that only you and your friends know. List words that you want to have gestures for. Or use phrases such as, "Let's get out of here," or "That's great." Now come up with movements to go with each one, such as pulling your ear or stroking your chin.

Once you've got the signals down, you can talk to one another without anyone else ever hearing a word.

# #363. CREATE a Moon Calendar

Did you ever notice how the moon keeps changing shape? One night it's a crescent, another night it's full—don't worry, it's just a phase. From here on Earth, the moon appears to change shape, going from no moon to crescent (sliver) to half-moon to full moon and gradually back to no moon. It takes about a month for the moon to go through all of these phases. Of course, the moon doesn't actually change shape. As the moon orbits Earth, we see more and more (or less and less) of the moon's bright face.

Track the moon's many shapes on your own moon calendar. Get a calendar that has boxes for each day with plenty of room for drawing. Every night go outside and look at the moon and draw its shape in that day's box. By the end of the month you will have seen the moon go through all its phases.

Changing the world sounds like a pretty tall order, but it's a lot easier than you might think.

If you simply be yourself, you will change the world. Being yourself means standing up for what you believe in, always trying to do your very best in everything, and treating others as well as you'd like to be treated. Just by doing these things, you've already made the world a better place.

You may never know when or how you are inspiring someone. If others see you trying to overcome something or finish a difficult task, you just might give them hope in their own struggles. If people know how much you care about issues and what goes on in your world, they'll take notice and begin to care, too. Speaking up about what you think is right is another easy way to change the world. Others may feel the same way you do, and by voicing your opinion you may give them the courage to speak, too.

The world is a great place, and it can be even greater—thanks to kids like you.

# #365. CREATE Your Own ADVENTURE

Don't wait for a book to tell you what to do; create your own adventure, and then go out and do it!

There are a lot of cool ideas in this book, but there are a ton more cool ideas inside your own head. Put your brain to work and come up with an incredible activity for you to do by yourself or with your friends.

Is there an animal that you wish you knew more about? Look it up! Is there a place you've always wanted to go? Plan a trip there! Are there any problems at your school that you'd like to see fixed? Don't just complain—do something about them. Have you always wanted to try something new or do things differently from the way you do them now? Go ahead and give it a shot.

Life is an adventure, so don't just read about it! Go out there and explore it all, try everything, experience as much as you can, and discover just how exciting your world really is.